P*** UP
IN A BREWERY

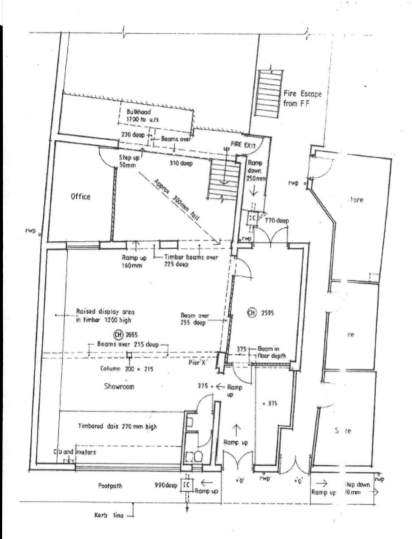

Stud parti
Floor to fl
of stairs(i
is approx.

Fire Escape
from F.F

Bulkhead
1700 to u/s

230 deep — Beams over

FIRE EXIT

Step up
50mm

310 deep

Ramp
down
250mm

Office

rwp

Approx 300mm fall

770 deep

rwp

Ramp up
160mm

Timber beams over
225 deep

Raised display area
in timber 1200 high

CH 2595

Beam over
255 deep

CH 2655

Beams over 215 deep

375 — Beam in
floor depth

Pier 'X'

Column 200 × 215

Showroom

375 ← Ramp
up

+ 375

Timbered dais 270 mm high

S re

C U and meters

Ramp up

Footpath

990 deep

Ramp up

rwp

Ramp up

Step down
0mm

Kerb line

Parking

Channel line

Existing Ground Floor Plan

P*** UP
IN A BREWERY

Tony Thomson

Scratching Shed Publishing Ltd

Typeset in Warnock Pro Semi Bold and Palatino
Printed and bound in the United Kingdom by

Trecerus Industrial Estate, Padstow,
Cornwall PL28 8RW
www.tjinternational.ltd.uk

Contents

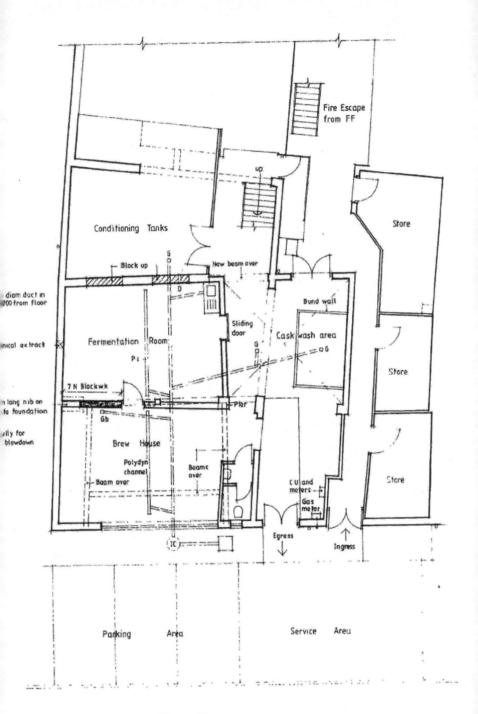

Proposed Ground Floor Plan

Glossary – A Few Brewing Terms

Conditioning: Also secondary fermentation or maturation. Unwanted flavours are purged from the beer and the CO2 level increases.

Crystal malt: Wet malt, heated rapidly, forms crystals in the grain. This adds colour and a sweet, toffee-like flavour.

Finings: Isinglass attaches to yeast particles and drags them to bottom, leaving beer clear.

Firkin: A 9-gallon container.

Gyle: Brew number.

Hogshead: 54-gallon container.

Keystone: A small wooden or plastic disc; completes the seal around the bung-hole of a cask.

Kilderkin: 18-gallon container.

Liquor: The water used to make the beer.

Mash: The mixture of malted grain and warm water in the mash tun.

Paraflow: Heat exchanger which cools the wort as it passes from the copper to the fermenting vessel.

Pin: A small cask, 4.5 gallons.

Pitching the yeast: Adding yeast (usually slurry) to the cooled wort in the fermenting vessel.

Pockets: 100kg bag of dried hops. A hop bale.

Racking: Filling casks.

Shive: Wooden or plastic fitting that plugs the hole on the upper side of a cask.

Skimming: Removing excess yeast from the top of the fermenting vessel.

Sparging: Spraying hot water on top of mash to help flush out sugars from the grain bed.

Sparkler: Device added to the nozzle of a beer engine to aerate the beer.

Spent grain: Remaining grain when the liquor wort has been drawn off after mashing.

Spile: A wooden peg placed in shive of a cask. Hard or soft.

Stillage: System of storing casks or barrels on their sides at a slight downward angle.

Torrefied grain: Grain that has been heated until it swells and bursts, rather like popcorn.

Tun: A large vessel.

Ullage: Originally meant the beer left in a barrel when it was finished with. Nowadays applied to all waste beer.

Underback: An intermediate vessel between mash tun and copper.

Wort: Sugary liquid extracted from the mash tun then added to the copper.

A Few of My Favourite Beers

I'm often asked what my favourite beer is. For the record, here's my top ten, excluding York Brewery's own brews.

1. **XXXB** 4.5 per cent, by George Bateman. A classic English brew, packed full of flavour. Batemans is a great story of survival.

2. **Brew York Brew York** 5 per cent, a new brewery in York, Les and Wayne have created a gem. York now has two great breweries to visit.

3. **Harvest Pale** 3.7 per cent and **Elsie Mo** 4.7 per cent. I'm allowing myself two here as they're both from Castle Rock. Great for a summer's day.

4. **White Star** 4.5 per cent from Titanic. Hoppy, but deceptively strong.

5. **Ruby Mild** 4.5 per cent. Rudgate get it right every time. Well worth a dabble.

6. **Tetley's Bitter** 3.7 per cent from Carlsberg, brewed at Banks' in Wolverhampton. I drank Tetley's at my local for years. When it was good it was 'proper good' – and the bell that rang for closing time was like the crack of doom.

7. **Strongarm** 4 per cent by Cameron's. Great balance of malt and hops. Best of the amber coloured bitters.

8. **Yankee** 4.3 per cent from Roosters of Knaresborough, the first small brewery to introduce canned beer.

9. **Theakston Best Bitter**, 3.8 per cent. Full-bodied, with five different hop varieties – a top brew.

10. **Leodis Lager** from Leeds Brewery. Yes, I have an interest, and yes, it's a lager, but their head brewer, Venks, is very good indeed.

Acknowledgements

Firstly, thanks to my co-writer Alan Wilkinson. I met him some years ago when he was living in York.

It was his love of a decent pint that brought him to the York Brewery (as member no. 752), and to celebrate his 60th birthday there. We devised a modus operandi that worked well for us. I wrote wads of material, longhand, and sent it off to Durham. He would return it a week or two later, suitably dressed up in fancy English and punctuated with long lists of questions.

Thanks are also due to Pete Hull, our cartoonist, John at Reprotek, and Rob at DC Graphics for their photographs.

Gavin Aitchinson from *The Press*, York, helped me retrieve articles and photographs from their archives.

Our beer consultant and adviser David Smith put us right on a number of technical matters. Then, of course, there are all the staff mentioned in the book, especially Nick Webster, Andrew Whalley, Alan Hardie, Barbara Vincent, Matt Moore, James Butler, Mandy Pegg and Mick Waite.

My brother Robin for his financial support, wisdom and belief. A stalwart ally, thanks bro.

Finally, my wife Julie, who put up with me shutting myself in my study for hours on end, then helping me unlock the creative process when I got stuck.

Dedication

For the girls in my life:
my wife Julie and my daughters Tessa, Emma and Alice,
whose support and encouragement gave
me much-needed motivation.

And for Smithy, my best mate, for sharing it all with me.

1.
NO QUESTION ABOUT IT, ALCOHOL WAS INVOLVED

There are two things to remember about good ideas. One is that they come at the most awkward times, usually when you're busy concentrating on the job in hand. The second is that just once in a while – once in a lifetime for most of us – that absolute cracker of an idea will show up out of the blue when you're scratching your head, wondering what life will throw at you next. When that happens, don't ask questions. Just grab it.

I was the wrong side of forty when it came to me. I was contemplating my imminent divorce, and the whacking great mortgage I had to pay, now that my ex had received her share of the equity in the house we once shared. £950 a month shouldn't have been beyond a Regional Director with a nationwide catering firm. The only problem was, I'd just been made redundant.

My wife had moved out a couple of years earlier, taking our three daughters with her. Certain that she'd return one

day, I'd let her keep a set of keys – which turned out very handy when she decided to come back and strip the house of all its furniture. She hadn't entirely lost her sense of fair play, however. She left me the television. Nor had she lost her sense of humour – she'd brought in a deck-chair from the garden and plonked it front of the telly. Maybe she wanted me to be comfortable. So I sat there, not very comfortable at all, and wondered. What next?

I decided that a beer might help. I got up, went into the kitchen and opened the fridge. Half a bottle of milk, a dried-up slab of cheese, three rubbery carrots – and no beer. I kicked the door shut and swore. Now, I'm not saying that was the moment I decided to start up my own brewery, but there's no question that beer was on my mind. I had this idea that it might help me forget the events of the past few months.

I'd been working for Rocco Forte for fifteen years. I'd risen to the giddy heights of Regional Director (North-east) with the Little Chef chain. One moment I was responsible for eighty restaurants, twenty Travel Lodges and a couple of garages; the next I was swept aside as if I were a blob of brown sauce spilled on one of their plastic-topped tables. The Region had been swallowed up in a re-organisation and disappeared from the map. I was surplus to requirements. Out on my ear.

The writing had been on the wall for some time. Shortly before the axe fell I'd had a meeting with the Purchasing Director at Head Office in Basingstoke. He was ablaze with enthusiasm over the firm's new sausage. It was small, perfectly formed, easy to cook, and it came from a reliable supplier. Better still, it was cheaper than any banger they'd ever had. It would cut the cost of the Full English and boost our profit margin.

'That's great,' I said. 'And the sausage itself… I mean, what's it like?' I can still see him, leaning forward over his desk and grinning as he said, 'Tony, that's the great thing. These sausages are almost edible!'

But never mind the bangers. What really stuck in my throat was the manner of my dismissal. Fair enough, Forte were trying to slim down their operation. These were tough times in the business, but they were hell bent on getting some of us old hands out without paying a compensation package. Someone in the upper echelons must have decided I was a suitable candidate. They delegated one of their bean-counters to sift through every transaction for which I'd ever claimed expenses. I could just imagine the glee with which he pounced on a £6 parking ticket.

There followed an almighty tussle, with threats of court action flying to and fro.

Thanks to a stout ally in H.R., I fought the charge and was promised a decent severance payment. £25,000. They got their pound of flesh, of course: they took back my company car, which I replaced with a Lada. £400, ugly as sin, but the seats matched my deck-chair.

So there I was: redundant, and middle-aged. I remember looking in the mirror one morning and realising that for the first time in my adult life I didn't need to get shaved. I had nowhere to go, nothing particular to do. I tried counting my blessings – just like they taught us in Sunday School. There was Alice, but she'd recently announced that she was now in a new relationship. We would remain good friends but it wouldn't be the same. I was missing her already. I scratched my head and, after giving it some thought, managed to come up with something to be grateful for. It was June, the sun was blazing down and England would be on the telly later, playing the West Indies at Lord's.

I grabbed a pile of trade magazines, took the deck-chair outside and sat in the sunshine browsing through them. Nothing. If there was a dream job out there with a boss I could respect, it wasn't being advertised this month. I threw them on the grass. In a way, I felt relieved. I knew I'd reached that age, that level of experience, where I was no longer cut out to do someone else's bidding. There was only one solution. I'd start my own business.

I sat there for some time, soaking up the sun. Then I picked up the bank statement that had arrived that morning. On the back of it I started to list the things I liked doing. I got as far as 'keeping wicket for Heslington Cricket Club' and 'going to the pub', then put the cricket on the TV. It was some hours later, during the tea interval, that my mate Kevin Nicholson showed up. I was still there, in my swimming shorts.

'Now then,' he said. 'Get some clothes on. We're going out.' 'Speak for yourself,' I said. 'I'm skint.' Then, as he plonked himself down on the grass, I asked, 'Out where, anyway?' 'We're going to visit a supplier of mine.' 'Yeah well, you go and enjoy yourself. I don't think I could stand the excitement.' 'This supplier I'm visiting,' he said, 'he has a micro-brewery.' 'Oh yeah?' I still wasn't really listening. I was wondering how Kevin and I had managed to end up in such very different situations.

We met not long after I'd got my A Level results, which were nothing to celebrate. Not like my genius brother, Robin, with his four grade As. I hadn't a clue what I was going to do with my life and was hanging around my parents' house in Markfield, Leicestershire, when I ran into a mate who was studying at Birmingham College of Food and Domestic Arts. 'They got this fantastic course,' he said. 'It's three girls to every bloke.' On such advice are whole careers built. I signed up, and that's where I bumped into Kevin. Together we staggered through a lot of parties, some epic pub crawls, a string of girlfriends, and three years of classes in Hotel Management. After graduating I spent the next few years running a number of pubs and restaurants before taking a job with Little Chef and climbing the corporate ladder. Life was a breeze.

Life had been kind to Kevin too: after spending some years in the RAF he'd landed on his feet and was now bursar for a couple of colleges at York University, just across the road from my house in Heslington village – the one I could no longer afford.

'Well,' he said, standing up and jingling his car keys, 'Time to be off. You coming?' 'I told you. I can't be going out on jollies. I've got things to do.' 'Such as?' 'Feeling sorry for myself.' 'But it's a brewery visit, Tony. These guys want me to stock their produce in the college bars.' He flicked a hand against my shoulder. 'Come on, we're talking quality beer here. And it's free.'

'Ah,' I said. 'That puts a different light on it.'

2.
'I CAN'T DRINK THIS!'

Kevin drove me out along the Scarborough road as far as Malton, then turned north. 'Not a hundred per cent sure where this place is,' he said as we entered Pickering. We turned up a narrow back lane, entered

Things are not always as they appear...

one of those bleak industrial estates – all concrete hard standing and chain-link fences – and drew up outside what looked like a large garage, or a small warehouse. 'This'll be it,' he said. It wasn't exactly John Smith's of Tadcaster, but it was the place we were looking for all right. There were casks outside and a sign over the door: 'Lastingham Brewery Company'.

Inside, we met a man in a white coat – slightly perturbing at first sight, given my depressed state of mind.

His name was Peter Frost, and this was his business. He had a long association with beer: his parents had the Blacksmith's Arms, a picturesque inn on the edge of the North York Moors at Lastingham – hence the name of his brewery.

He showed us around. The whole place was sparkling. It was cleaner than a hospital. The floors were scrubbed and all the metalwork was gleaming. There was an interesting smell in the air, sort of yeasty. There were various bubbling noises. In a corner was a stack of barrels.

As Peter talked us through the brewing process I was struck by his evident passion for his job – and his beer. By the time he'd finished his enthusiasm for his product had me drooling in anticipation. I was gagging for a pint. He grabbed a couple of glasses, went to the corner and filled one for Kevin, another for me. This was the moment I'd been waiting for. Cask conditioned ale, straight from the source. I held my pint up to the light, then screwed up my nose and said, 'I can't drink this.'

Thinking back, I can't come up with a single reason why our host didn't land one on me there and then - or invite me to leave the premises. But all he said was, 'What's the matter with it?' He looked sort of hurt.

'Why, it's cloudy,' I said. 'Look at it. I can't even see my fingers through the glass.' If he'd been the type, he could have made me feel small and stupid. Instead, he addressed me as a kindly, patient teacher might address a rather dim child. 'That,' he said, 'is because it hasn't been fined yet.'

'Fined?' He'd got me there. The only fines I'd come across were ones I'd picked up for speeding along the A64.

'Beer is naturally cloudy,' he said. 'It's the yeast. Won't do you any harm, but people want a nice clear pint, don't they?' I nodded. What else was I to do? 'So you add finings to get rid of it,' he said. 'We use isinglass.'

'Isinglass?' It wasn't a word I was familiar with.

'Yes, it's an interesting product,' he said. 'It's found in the flotation bladder of the sturgeon. It has the very useful property of attracting the yeast particles. Forms them into little clots that sink to the bottom, leaving you with a nice clear pint.' He laughed, then said, 'Why do you think they drank out of tankards in the old days?'

I shrugged my shoulders.

'So that people wouldn't see it was cloudy. To be fair, it can put you off. If you're ignorant, that is.' I could've sworn I saw him wink at Kevin as he said that.

'Ah,' I said, 'sorry.' I closed my eyes, raised the glass to my mouth and tilted my head back.

That was the light-bulb moment. Peter's brew – I can't recall its name, but it was some kind of pale ale – was absolutely delicious. It had taste, character, body and… well, there was something else, but I was already draining the glass and struggling to find the word. I was pretty sure my taste-buds were about to burst into song. 'So this,' I purred, 'this is what beer's supposed to taste like?'

'Precisely,' said our host. 'Fancy another?'

I did, and as it slipped down I took a second look around the place. There really wasn't much of it. It was no bigger than a decent-sized restaurant kitchen.

'Why so small?' I asked. 'I mean, why aren't you cranking this stuff out by the ship-load?' He didn't answer the question as such, but he did tell me that most of his product went to a pub he owned in Leeds.

I later learned that Peter's pub was in a part of the town where drug-dealers were operating. When the police asked him if they could use the premises overnight to stake out the area, he obliged.

8

What was effectively the sole outlet for his brew was burned down a few days later. It was pretty obvious that it was no accident – and that he should have diversified. But by then it was too late.

'Yeah but, how much are you making?' I asked. 'Beer like this – I mean, it should be everywhere.' I drained the glass. 'Every pub in the country. You should be selling this the length and breadth of England. It's fantastic.' I watched as he topped me up again. Kevin declined; he was driving.

Peter seemed pleased with my response to his beer. Maybe that's why he didn't tell me about the many hurdles erected by the major breweries, and the pub chains, to keep out the small operator. Looking back, I'm glad he didn't. Very glad. It would have made me think twice.

Kevin didn't say a lot as he drove us back to York. He couldn't. I was off on one, slagging off every big-name beer I could think of, fantasising about a life as a brewer and how we could conquer the world with this fabulous product.

P*** Up In A Brewery

We left Kevin's car off at the Uni and legged it to the village. Heslington had two pubs. There was the Deramore Arms, and the Charles XII, both of them three minutes from my house. Far too handy. 'Get them in,' Kevin said, 'You're two pints ahead of me.'

It didn't take him long to catch up. He had nothing else to do for the rest of the evening except sit and drink beer and agree with me, nodding silently as I built castles in the air. By the time the landlord showed us the door I had it all worked out. I would create my own brewery in York, set up a chain of pubs and take the industry by storm. As the money rolled in I'd probably sponsor a Test Match series, and spend my retirement drawing fat dividends while watching the cricket from a private box.

The miracle was that next morning, as I nursed a vicious hangover and thought over the previous night, I still liked my idea. As I waited for my tea to brew I picked up a pencil and started to write down the reasons why this was the way forward for me.

Don't put all your eggs in one basket...

Number 1, there was no brewery in the city of York, and hadn't been since 1954 when Camerons bought up Hunts. They closed it down two years later. The Federation or working men's clubs brewery operated until the 1970s, but it didn't count. It was out at Huntington. I wasn't sure how I knew all that, but I did. Probably some old codger in the Charles belly-aching about how things used to be. I chewed on my pencil and wrote, Number 2: York could do with its own brewery. Then I realised that was covered by item 1. It wasn't much of a list, but the idea was still a cracker.

I rang Kevin's office a few minutes later. I needed to hear him confirm my opinion. He was gentle but firm.

'Tony, you're gonna have to lower your voice. I'm in pain.' Then he said, 'Listen, you kept talking about 'we' yesterday. Before you say another word I'm going to tell you right now there's no way I'm going to leave a secure, well-paid job – even one I don't like – and partner you in a suicide mission, because that's what starting up a brewery is. Absolute kamikaze. You do know that, don't you?'

I was too stunned to stop him. Instead I listened as he spelled it out. 'What you need to realise is, the failure rate of micro-breweries is up there with the failure rate of... I dunno…' He was struggling here for a moment; then he said, 'It's on a par with first marriages, that's what it is.' And who was I to argue with that?

So Kevin wasn't going to partner me. But never mind. I was pretty sure I knew a man who would.

3.
MUST HAVE G.S.O.H. – AND MORE MONEY THAN SENSE

When you decide to go into business with a partner you need to weigh your options very carefully indeed. It's probably a tougher decision than choosing a wife – or a husband. Whoever you go for has to be hard-working. If they're going to dedicate several years of their life to the project – and I'm talking about fifteen- and eighteen-hour days, six days a week, sometimes seven – he or she must have absolute belief in the scheme. Total faith.

Choose your partner with care, it's the most important decision you'll make

On top of that your other half needs to excel in all the areas where you're lacking. (We'll get to my failings later.) Intelligence and a sense of humour we can count as given. The next crucial attribute is versatility. It's an interesting word that. What it means is, your partner really will turn their hand to absolutely anything – including the most menial tasks. I learned early on that you can always spot the directors in a new business: they're the ones cleaning out the toilets. Throw in a facility for multi-tasking, a delight in taking huge risks and a gift for motivating others; add limitless patience, an acute eye for detail, a capacity for taking criticism and a tolerance of all your failings, and we're getting there. Then consider the question, is this a person I like and respect? If so, there's only one more question: how much can they afford to invest? No, hang on a minute; I've forgotten something. Where the hell do you find such a person?

I see I haven't mentioned luck. When it came to seeking a partner – more accurately described as someone willing to accept half the blame when things go wrong – I didn't really have to look very far. I knew who I wanted. It was a man I'd known for many, many years.

I started out with Little Chef as a Regional Manager. It sounds grand. My wife was impressed, initially. I was in my late twenties when I met her, and she was young – still doing her A levels, in fact. I was running a theatre bar and working evenings and weekends. She wanted a social life. So I promised her that I'd get out of the licensed trade and leave its unsocial hours behind.

Think frying-pans and fires. In my new job my feet never touched the ground. I began with three months of training. After a brief induction period and a two-week crash-course in management they had me running a Little Chef at Alwalton, on the A1, followed by a month shadowing another area manager up in Scotland.

Scotland was fun. Or rather, it gave me a few laughs. The guy I was sent out with was another Tony. Henderson, they called him. He knew all the dodges. On our first day out together we had to call on a farmer to get permission to put a billboard on his land. A roadside hoarding, Tony assured me, could easily add 10 per cent to your customer numbers.

It was a foul day, the rain coming in horizontally. Bitterly cold too. We pulled off the road and into a farmyard. 'Okay,' my mate said, 'just nip over and tap on his door, will you?' I was wearing standard management dress, a smart new Jaeger blazer and a pair of freshly ironed grey slacks. I'd polished my black shoes to within an inch of their life. The yard was ankle-deep in cow-shit.

'You must be joking,' I said. 'Look at me. And anyway, it's your sign.' Tony grinned. 'Yeah okay,' he said, grabbing a crumpled kagool from the back. 'Just thought I'd give it a try.'

I watched through his open door as he splashed his way through the mire. As he disappeared into the murk a huge, scruffy border collie bounded past him, leapt into his seat and attacked me. I don't mean 'attacked' as in 'started chewing lumps out of me'. No, this dog fancied me. He – or it may have been a she – seemed to be showering me with affection – and mud; and cow-crap, and dog-slobber. My shoes, my clothes, my face, my hands – and the shiny seat of Tony's company car - were lathered in it. I did manage to laugh – but not until several weeks had elapsed.

Tony was all about sales. And he had some interesting theories as to what drew people into a Little Chef – leaving aside the fact that half the time the average motorist had no choice. There were precious few roadside cafés in rural Scotland at that time.

'Now, this place,' he said, as we drew into a branch for a stock-take one afternoon, 'this place gets a ton of customers – but only on certain shifts. See if you can work out why.'

It didn't take long. The supervisor on duty was a lovely looking lass, with a great figure and a lovely pair of breasts.

And, this being the seventies, she didn't wear a bra. Just her standard-issue white blouse which, like many things Little Chef, was made of insubstantial material. To put it plainly, she had all the goods on display, and neither of us was going to suggest she change a thing: her sales figures would suffer.

She wasn't the only one who posed such a problem. The supervisor at Nuthill was also averse to wearing a bra. When I explained to her, as delicately as I could, that the company had a 'no-nipple' policy, she made it clear that she was up to speed on current fashions and I was living in the Dark Ages. Next time I went to check on her, however, she'd gone. The staff showed me her press cuttings. She was the daughter of Viv *Spend Spend Spend* Nicholson, the legendary pools-winner from Castleford, and she'd just run off with her mother's latest husband.

After my baptism of fire north of the border, I was pretty much ready to go it alone in the north-east. I'd been in post about a week when I got a call from the manager at Bramham Crossroads, where the A64 from Leeds to Scarborough crossed the Great North Road, as we knew it then. It was branch number 207. These are the kinds of detail you remember. Sometimes you wish you didn't, but you do.

'I've got a question for you,' she said. 'Fire away.' 'Can I re-employ someone I've just sacked?' Great, I thought. Just what I want. But I knew what to do. Answer a question with another one. That usually works. 'What did you sack him for?' I asked. 'He told me to, er – well, if you want it in plain English he told me to fuck off.' 'Really? And you want him back?' 'Oh hell yes.' 'Why?' 'Two reasons. I'm desperate for staff, and this lad's the best griddle cook I've ever seen. He is a phenomenon.' I gave it a bit of thought, then said, 'Okay. I'll trust you on this. But when I call by be sure to introduce him to me. I'll have a quiet word about his behaviour.'

The chance came a few days later. Tony Smith was quite a bit younger than me, say twenty years old. He wasn't what you'd call a looker, and that was an issue in itself: our chefs did their work in full view of the customers, right behind the counter. He was built like a stick insect – I mean a not very well nourished stick insect; he had appalling facial acne, and his teeth, those that weren't missing, were a nightmare. I sat him down for a chat, and that's when I discovered his other failing. He was incapable of uttering four consecutive words without throwing in a 'bloody' or a 'bleeding'. It was pathological; like a speech impediment.

Fortunately for him, there was a 'however' – and to be fair there needed to be. What came through in that interview was the lad's genuine passion for his job. He was crazy about it, and so long as he was at his hot-plates he was in seventh heaven. To hear him wax lyrical about the bleedin' bacon, or the bloody sausages, or the sodding eggs, was to hear a man in love. In love with fried breakfasts, toast, bangers... with all things Little Chef.

It would be years later that I heard Smithy's version of

what had happened when the manager fired him, his assertion that the manageress was a schizoid psychopath – and his admission that, as he sat at home next day, he found himself thinking, 'Shit, I miss the place.'

But then Tony was a lad who always called a spade a bloody shovel. He once told me how he dealt with a particularly awkward customer, a woman who insisted on being served a beefburger, even after he'd told her several times there were none in stock and she could have anything else she fancied, free. She worked herself up into such a fury that all the other customers stopped eating and just stared at her. She wanted a burger and it was Tony's job, as manager, to provide one. In the end he lost it. 'So what is it?' he asked. 'You want me to go out and shoot a fucking cow?'

Over the next few years I backed Tony as he was promoted to Supervisor at Bramham, to Deputy Manager at Nuthill, to Manager at Bardon Mill on the A69, and some of the busiest outlets, like Shiptonthorpe on the York-Hull road. Shiptonthorpe was phenomenally busy. I once had a manageress there, a woman called Margaret Baxter, who called me after a storm to say that the roof had blown off. I thought she had to be exaggerating, but when I showed up I found the entire structure laid out in the car-park, the café itself exposed to the skies. But it was full of customers, and normal service was being maintained. 'What was I going to do?' she asked, 'turn them away?' Margaret was very old school. When Tony Smith called in one time he found two large jam pans on the griddle and air thick with an unappetising smell. She was boiling up the tea towels.

But then Little Chef seemed to attract what you'd call characters. I once had cause to ask a manager how he managed to keep his wage-bill so low. You only had to glance at his figures for it to leap off the page. He confided – I should say he confessed – that his waiters were paying school-kids, thirteen- and fourteen-year-olds, 50p an hour out of their tips to help them with their work. Full marks for initiative, but it contravened all kinds of employment laws and had to stop.

Later, when I became Regional Director, Tony became my Commercial Manager. Before long I promoted him to Regional Manager. By this time his acne had cleared up and, after endless visits to the dentist, he'd got a decent set of teeth. The swearing? It seemed that was part of the package. He tried valiantly, but he only made a marginal improvement. Still, he'd grown up on a run-down housing estate in an impoverished area of Leeds. His first job was putting arms and legs onto Lucky Bears in a toy factory in Wetherby. He'd joined Little Chef as a dish-washer. So he wasn't doing badly, at all. People liked him. They valued him. They accepted him for what he was – namely, a great guy. They also recognised that he had a sharp business brain. He was great with figures, budgeting, forecasts; and, like so many Yorkshiremen, he was a skinflint: he simply hated spending money. Quite a profile for a potential business partner.

When I was made redundant, Tony naturally wanted to know what the hell I was going to do. I told him I'd no idea, but I thought I might set up my own business. 'Really?' he said. 'Well, let me know if you need me.' Tony was getting pretty fed up with Little Chef by this time. After having one sick-day in fourteen years, he now declared himself unfit and stayed off for some time, on full pay, and made regular visits to York, where we chewed the fat.

Shortly after the visit to Lastingham's I called Tony and invited him over to York. I told him we were going to have a few beers, then adjourn to my favourite Indian restaurant, the Viceroy. I had a plan, and it worked to perfection. I took him to a pub just outside the city walls, the Tap and Spile on

Monkgate. Back then the Tap was one of the few pubs in the city that served cask conditioned or 'real' ales – but the fact is, what they were offering wasn't exactly top-grade. In fact, it was crap. Not that Tony would know. He had obviously done something unspeakably bad in a previous life and had come back to earth as a lager-drinker. I ordered a couple of pints of their guest ale, which I already knew was past its best. 'Try that,' I said.

He looked at the dark brew through narrowed eyes. 'What the bloody hell is it?' he asked, leaning forward to sniff it. 'Cask ale, mate. As opposed to that shite they serve out of kegs. It's the coming thing. Everyone's drinking it. Go on, sup up.' He picked it up, then tilted his head back and downed about a third of a pint. 'Bloody hell, Tony!' He slammed his glass on the bar. 'That is bleeding horrible. What you trying to do, bloody poison me?' I had to feel sorry for the guy. He looked genuinely hurt. 'That,' he said, shaking his head, 'is bloody disgusting.'

Keep a record of your ideas, however weird. One day they might make sense

'Exactly,' I said. And I leaned towards him. 'So you and me, we could surely do a sight better, don't you think?'

He looked puzzled. 'I don't get it,' he said. 'Let me explain,' I said. 'We are going to start up our own brewery.'

Smithy answered as Smithy would. 'You must be fucking joking,' he said. Then it dawned on him that I was deadly serious. 'Fetch us another pint,' he said. 'Lager.'

We had another drink or two, then adjourned to the Viceroy, just across the road. This was and still is my favourite curry house in York. Mahmood, Rocky and Naz have looked after me and my guests there for over thirty years. We sat down and I outlined my plan, such as it was. Smithy said he'd have a think.

I didn't hear from him for a few days, during which I convinced myself that he was dead against the idea – and that I was deluding myself. Or that it had got lost in an alcoholic haze. Then, one evening after work, he called round at my house. 'Okay,' he said, 'I'm in.' Maybe it was the mad gleam in my eye. Maybe it was loyalty to me. More likely it was the Little Chef factor. He was, he admitted, fed up to the back teeth with them, and ready for a new challenge.

We went across the road to the Charles XII and did what everybody who starts up a new business ends up doing. Writing lists. And that's what we did for several weeks. I would write a list, he would write one, and we'd meet up and compare them. Then we'd write a new one. Sometimes we'd go to the Deramore for a change and write different lists, and cross out half the stuff we'd put on the previous ones.

If I learned one thing at this stage it was not to throw out the old lists as we produced new ones. Somewhere, buried away in all the rejects, might be that crucial idea whose time hadn't yet come.

4.
I SERVED MY TIME –
MOSTLY BEHIND BARS

I'm making it sound as though I wandered into the brewery business on a whim. The fact is, I had a long history, prior to working at Little Chef, in the business of selling beer – and, of course, drinking it.

When I was a student, I spent far too much time in various Birmingham alehouses. We all did. Most of my grant – remember them? – passed across the counter in the Shakespeare Arms, and I recouped my losses working evening shifts at the bar of the Alexandra Theatre. I certainly made my mark there. We had Ronnie Corbett playing in panto, and I managed to pour a full glass of red wine all down his white dress shirt. I also worked as a waiter in the Opposite Lock Night Club. On quiet nights our chef used to amuse himself by sending new kitchen porters off to the canal side with a kids' fishing-net and telling them to fetch back a bit of whitebait. Some of them seemed genuinely disappointed when they didn't catch any.

P*** Up In A Brewery

After I graduated, with the letters HCIMA after my name, I headed south and got a job at the Bell House Hotel in Beaconsfield, one of the De Vere group. This was a big place with two banqueting suites. As the assistant banqueting manager I was put in charge of the smaller one, which seated 200. I didn't last long. Nothing to do with my capabilities, just the hours we had to keep. The manager was a proper party animal. He'd regularly have us back to his room after work, all the management in their dress suits. For reasons best known to him, we drank Scotch and milk and played cards – his favourite game being shoot pontoon. He'd keep us at it until breakfast time, when we'd go down, grab some breakfast and start the day's work.

It was basic sleep deprivation that cost me my driving licence. Well, that and excessive drinking. I was driving home in the early hours, when I simply nodded off at the wheel. When I regained consciousness the car was upside down in someone's front garden. I was some feet away on the lawn. The occupants were hovering around us in their dressing-gowns. I wasn't hurt, but the car was. When the police showed up they took one look at the tyres and said, 'Looks as though you have a tread problem, sir.' Then they breathalysed me. I was totally relaxed about that. Why should I worry? I hadn't had a drink since the party the night before last. I learned something valuable that night, about how long alcohol can stay in your system. It turned out I'd had enough to leave a substantial trace in my blood thirty-six hours later. So that was me, banned for twelve months.

The Bell House was a fun place to be, so long as you could get by on next to no sleep. We had a pretty good football team – some staff, but mainly a bunch of talented players who drank in our trendy public bar. Rod Stewart, who once had trials with Brentford FC, had been among them, but around the time of my arrival his musical career was taking off so I never got the chance to kick a ball around with the born-again Scotland supporter. I wasn't a bad player myself in those days and was once approached by the manager of Slough Town of the Isthmian League. Did I want to go and play for them? There would be a few quid in it. I might have given it a go, but at the same time I got an offer of work from the manager of the Hillingdon Motel, just a few miles along the A40.

I had one or two regrets about leaving The Bell House. One was the head receptionist, Di, who happened to be the assistant manager's wife. She'd taken a fancy to me, and made me promise to stay in touch. However, Hillingdon – and the chance to catch up on some shut-eye – was calling.

As many have said, before and since, in all kinds of circumstances, the move to Hillingdon seemed a good idea at the time. It appeared to be a forward step: I was to be deputy manager, and the position came with a flat on top of the motel. The disadvantage, of course, was that I was living over the shop and would be on call twenty-four seven. But those were the least of my worries. As soon as I started working with my new manager I realised I was in trouble. The guy wasn't much older than me; he was arrogant, and lazy. Those weren't his only failings, but it took a little time for me to see right through him. They called him Mister Churchill – to his face. Behind his back he was Mister Fucking Churchill.

We got off to a great start. 'Okay,' he said, after he'd shown me my room, 'your first job. I want all the bar staff sacked.'

'When?' I said.

He looked at his watch. 'Soon as they come on duty,' he said. 'Which will be in ten minutes.'

'Can I ask what they've done?' He was already on his way back to his office, and I was trailing along behind him. 'It's the wet stock,' he said, over his shoulder. 'There's drinks going missing, and I'm getting it in the neck from head office.'

'Okay,' I said, 'but who's going to run the bar once we've fired them?'

'You are.'

The place was a total shambles. The staff turnover was so rapid you never knew who half the people were – and in any case we were always short-handed. Even the table settings told a tale, the glasses dirty and the cutlery mismatched. The good news was that Mister Churchill was mostly absent. Everything he knew about what was going on he got from his head receptionist, a nasty, hard-faced woman who took an instant dislike to me. I kept my head down and tried to avoid the manager. I had an awful feeling I was going to have to kill him. I knew right away that I wouldn't be staying for long, but any move would have to wait until I got my driving licence back.

Fortunately, my relationship with the manager soon improved. He told me he was concerned about the food stocks. It wasn't just the drinks that were going missing, he said; someone was nicking the grub, and I needed to sort it out. A day or two later I was grabbing a few minutes' rest in what I liked to call my penthouse. I happened to look out of the window and noticed a light on in the kitchen, which I'd just locked. I went to investigate, and found the manager in there, filling up a big box with steak, whole chickens, cheeses and other goodies. He was as nice as pie to me from then on.

If I thought that Hillingdon was a baptism of fire, my next job re-defined the term. John Kenny, an old college friend, had been in touch, trying to persuade me to join a fledgling company he was involved with. 'You can start off running this hotel,' he said. 'It's in Lowestoft.' I agreed without asking any further questions. Anything had to be better than this lousy motel, and here was a job by the seaside; it sounded great.

As soon as I told Di I was heading for the wilds of East Anglia she came over all wistful and confided that she and her husband were now officially separated. She looked at me and asked, straight out, 'So… can I come with you?'

The Crown Hotel was a real man's pub. It was a hang-out for serious boozers, some of them with a psychotic strain. I didn't know why the previous manager had departed, but there was a clue in the dog he left behind. Victor was a German Shepherd, probably deranged. When I showed up he wouldn't let me in, just hurled himself at the door, barking and snarling with his chops all covered with drool. Somehow I got him into the yard, which I then locked. As he got hungrier he calmed down a little. It took several days, but slowly it dawned on him that if he was going to eat he would have to be nice to me. From that point on he turned on the charm and we got along just fine.

The Crown was a hotel in name only. Most of the rooms hadn't been inhabited in years. A few were taken by the live-in staff, which consisted of me and Di, our new head chef Billy – another veteran of the Bell House – and the public room barman, a fellow named Reg.

My first few nights the place seemed easy enough to manage. There weren't a great many customers, the dog was under control, and Reg was whistling a happy tune. Reg was a big fellow, broad in the chest, tall, and with a seriously ugly face: squashed nose, cauliflower ears, that sort of thing. He was a bruiser. When I first set eyes on him I remember thinking I probably wouldn't have employed him. Nothing wrong with his skills, just that I wouldn't want him to be the

first thing the punters saw when they walked in. He looked the sort of guy who might frighten the regulars – and I was right. Most of them lived in mortal dread of him.

It was an odd sort of place, the Crown. I mean, how many pubs do you walk into and find a large fish-pond sunk into the floor, slap-bang in the middle of the bar? Whoever had put it there must have thought it gave the place some sort of quaint atmosphere. Or a touch of class. Think Las Vegas, with all the weirdness and none of the glitz. There was a myna bird too.

It was called Max, and was in the habit of sitting on Victor's shoulder. The rumour was that he came from the pet-shop across the road. The owner had run up a sizeable tab, couldn't afford to settle it, and offered the bird as part payment. I made it my ambition to teach Max to talk, but all I ever got was a hideous squawk. I remember the day I came into the bar and found Billy looking at the floor, where Max lay, beak partly open, utterly lifeless. 'What happened?' I asked. He shrugged. 'Nae idea,' he said, 'he just keeled over.' 'That's a shame,' I said. 'I was hoping to get him talking.'

Billy's humour was as dark and impenetrable as the remote part of Scotland he came from – somewhere quite unpronounceable. He looked at me and said, 'Aye. Funny you should mention that, Tony. Because he did say one thing before he died.' 'He did?' 'Aye, he gasped, "bi-ird seed", then over he went.'

As to our regular customers, a lot of them were off the fishing-boats. They'd come in together – a captain, a mate and a rough-looking crew, most of them recruited from Norwich Prison. The skippers literally went up to the jail and hung around outside the gates waiting for people to be discharged at a certain time of day. Many of them were desperate for work and willing to accept lousy pay and terrible conditions. Quite a few, having no experience of life at sea, were lost overboard.

Mad Mick, however, was no sailor. One of our regulars in the public bar, he was just a genuine Suffolk nutter, an unreconstructed Teddy Boy who wore tight jeans, a long purple jacket and crepe-soled brothel-creepers. Normally he behaved quite well, they told me. It was just when he'd had a drink, they said. It's not what a pub landlord wants to hear. My first encounter with him came when I followed a trail of blood to the toilet and found him picking bits of glass out of his hand. It seemed he'd crushed a goblet in his fist. On the way out he smashed a wall-light for good measure. 'Right,' I said, taking my courage in my hands, 'I want you out of here.'

It seemed to work. Mick barged through the glazed doors and lurched out into the street. As he walked away I called after him, 'And don't come back – you hear?'

I was pushing my luck and I knew it. Mick turned around and started running towards me. My God, he was a frightening sight. I closed my eyes and swung the door shut. There was an almighty crash, and there was Mick, doubled over, blood dripping from his hand, and my barmaid staring at a large round hole in the glass. 'What happened?' I asked.

'He put his fist through it,' she said. 'He was trying to hit you.'

If I thought the Crown was rough, I was about to discover that it was a haven of sanity compared with the other places where Lowestoft's lowlife gathered to drink, fight and kill off their remnant brain cells. The damage to the Crown's doors was substantial, and in order to claim on the pub's insurance I would need a police incident number. I put in a call and told them what had happened. They showed up soon after, two of them in a squad car. We went to the pub next door where, we understood, our man had been drinking before he decided to grace us with his presence. Had he caused any trouble in there? Nothing out of the ordinary, they told us. Just downed a treble rum and threw up in the ash-tray.

'Come on, we'll take a look around town, shall we?' the senior cop said. And so I embarked on a tour of Lowestoft's dark under-belly, entering pubs I'd never heard of and never wished to visit again. We didn't find our man, but the two hours I spent in those dives gave me a new appreciation of the Crown's merits.

Mick wasn't the only nutter amongst our regulars. He was just, by a small margin, the worst. On a typical Friday night he would hardly stand out amongst a whole cast of boozing, fighting, crazies. My first weekend, I came down to find Reg entering the bar with Victor on a heavy chain, which he anchored to an iron ring set in the floor by the cellar entrance. I watched, in silence as he reached into a murky corner and pulled out a length of timber. It was four inches by four and one end of it was marked with dark, sinister-looking stains. Reg laid it on the bar top, slipped off his coat and rolled up his shirt-sleeves.

'What's going on?' I asked. 'What you doing all that for?'

I dare say he tried to hide his contempt for his new boss, but I don't think he tried very hard. He turned down the corners of his mouth and said, 'Friday night, isn't it?' then took off his watch and placed it in the till. He was a man of few words.

I didn't take him seriously. I saw no reason to. My first customers were four gorgeous looking young women, all done up in their glad-rags. 'Yes,' I greeted them, all smiles and trying not to stare too hard at their exposed bosoms, 'what'll it be?'

One of them stared at me through a haze of cheap perfume and lacquered hair, curled a scarlet lip and said, 'Four pints, cunt.'

By ten o'clock I was thanking my lucky stars that Reg was there – and making sure that he was always standing between me and the mob of heavyweights pressed against the bar holding out empty glasses and snarling out their orders while, behind them, discussions about football and women turned into arguments, then into fights, and the fists started flying. Fists, glasses, bottles – and the occasional carp, from the fish-pond.

I survived six months at the Crown, during which the police were regular visitors. That was no surprise, really, seeing that they had a training college in town. Mostly when I called for help the local constabulary would whistle up the cadets, then resume their game of cards. It was a mixed

blessing. We'd get a bus-load of young coppers, eager to earn a few credits and practise their newly acquired skills in unarmed combat. That generally meant that as soon as they'd sorted out the first fight another would break out between them and the combined locals. I remember a weary constable surveying the wreckage in the bar one night after another free-for-all. He asked me, 'Look, you don't want us putting you out of business, do you?' I looked him right in the eye and replied, 'To be honest, I wish you would, mate. I really do.'

In the periodic lulls, which lasted from Monday to Thursday, I decided I ought to try to increase the takings. I had one bright idea, a pool table. Reg was dead against it. 'They won't stand for it,' he said. By 'they' he meant the regulars. 'They're here to drink beer. They don't want no distractions. Most likely wreck it.'

I persisted. 'Yeah, but think of all those coins being shoved in hour after hour,' I said. He rolled his eyes and left me to it. I was the boss, and I would carry the can.

The pool table was my first successful innovation, but,

this being the Crown, there were problems. From their initial posture – any change was a change for the worse – the pub regulars slowly came to see this as a genius move. They flocked around the table. They started a league, and a knock-out competition. They arranged games against other pub teams. They placed bets. This was great. Suddenly they had something else to fight about. They couldn't get enough of it. And when a big match was on they turned a deaf ear to the clanging of the bell for last orders and my lame attempts to send them out into the night. In despair I turned to Reg, who shrugged his shoulders, unhooked Victor's leash and set the big brute loose. When he landed on the table, it was as if a small explosive device had been set off. Balls, cues, pint glasses and players were scattered in all directions – but at least we were then left to sweep up the debris in peace.

Prior to my installing the pool table, the only money-maker in the place was a jukebox.

It was popular, so popular in fact that if you wanted to hear the latest by Slade, or Gilbert O'Sullivan or, God help us, Little Jimmy Osmond, (this was 1972, and it really was that bad) you needed to get your ten pence in early and hope you'd make it to the top of the queue by closing time.

Needless to say, you can't please all of the people all of the time, and when drinking-up time was over, and the lights were full on, the windows and doors wide open, there was always some drunken female clinging to the jukebox, waiting for her favourite to come blasting out – and as often as not some muscle-bound oik clinging to her in anticipation of a knee-trembler on the way home. It was my job to turn the thing off. I tried it once and was told in no uncertain terms to 'Get that fucking volume up.' I called Victor out and let him loose. He pinned the offender against the wall and breathed foul breath right into the lad's face. In the end I moved the volume control to a spot behind the bar and, once I'd called last orders, turned it down in stages.

The pub, I learned, was owned by a company being set up by a fellow named Dutton. He was a bit of a whizz-kid, a graduate of Harvard; and he'd just come from establishing the Pizza Hut chain. He summoned me to a meeting, and explained his plans to upgrade the Crown and turn it into a thing of wonder. I didn't take him seriously until a gang of builders arrived with instructions to convert our spacious entrance lobby into an upscale kind of lounge bar. They made a pig's ear of it. It was a cheap and nasty conversion. The walls buckled if you leant too hard on them, and you could hear the jukebox right through them. It might as well have been in the same room.

I started to get the impression that this place wasn't going to work out for me. I realised I wasn't the only one the day I received a phone call tipping me off that the new M.D. was going to sack us all. He thought we weren't making enough sales.

Well, they say the best form of defence is attack. I wrote out a resignation letter for myself and Di, kept a copy, and made sure it was dated the day before I got the tip-off. When the head honcho showed up next day and told us we were fired due to poor sales I had the satisfaction of telling him he was too late, and had he checked the morning post. As he stood there blinking at me, I whipped out my copy of the resignation letter.

When Di and I drove off, with Victor in the back of the car – the big daft animal had fallen for us big time – it was with huge relief.

We went to my parents' place in Markfield and took it easy for a few days, during which I looked up my old mate from school, Neil Spiers. He and I had hitch-hiked to Greece

together as sixteen-year-olds to visit my Aunt Eve, who was living and working in Athens back then.

Neil had landed a decent job at the Nottingham Playhouse, being their Licensee and Catering Manager. As soon as he learned that we were free he said, 'How about coming and working for me? There's a fair chance of something interesting coming up in the near future, and you'll be in pole position. D'you fancy it?' Did I fancy it? If ever there was a time to ask whether the Pope wore a funny hat, this was it.

5.
BRIAN CLOUGH, DEREK RANDALL AND RICHARD EYRE: NOTTINGHAM IN THE 1970s WAS THE PLACE TO BE

I soon found out what was going on. Neil and his assistant were branching out on their own, buying a pub, and Neil saw me as the ideal replacement for him. He said he'd have a word with his Area Manager, a fellow called Dennis Bennett. Dennis worked for Ansells the brewers, who had the concession to run the bar and catering side.

Once I started work, I hardly saw Neil. He was too busy sorting out his new enterprise. He more or less left me to my own devices, and I rose to the challenge. Then I got word that Dennis wanted to see me. He turned out to be a wonderfully laid-back guy: bright, witty and a real motivator. I couldn't have asked for a better boss. He told me that Neil was on his way and his position was available. He interviewed me for about half an hour, after which he asked me, 'Have you got your keys?' 'Yeah, sure.' 'Is there anything you need to know?' 'I don't think so. I've been running the place on my own for two months.' 'Great, the job's yours.'

I was to have several happy years in Nottingham, along with an intensive education on the paperwork side of management. Which I needed, because it soon became apparent to me that I didn't know a lot – and Dennis was rarely around to help me. He had some twenty pubs to look after in the Nottingham-Derby-Leicester area. One of them, just along the road from us, was the famous Trent Bridge Inn, right by the cricket ground. It was managed by a proper local character called Norman Mee, whose name crops up in the memoirs of Test Match umpire Dickie Bird. Norman used to invite the other managers onto the roof during Test Matches. They had a great view from up there, and I was privileged to watch, horrified, as Geoffrey Boycott, playing his first Test for three years, ran out local hero Derek Randall in an Ashes Test.

Nottingham at that time was a prestigious venue, quite a landmark on England's theatrical map – not that I knew anything about that. In fact, I was profoundly ignorant of the subject. There was an up-and-coming director in charge at the Playhouse, but nobody bothered to introduce me to him. I soon found out who he was. I'd gone down to the cellar to change a keg of lager and found this total stranger stumbling about, helping himself to the vintage Bordeaux.

'Who the hell are you?' I asked. 'No,' he replied, 'who the hell are you?' I told him I was the boss, and he introduced himself as Richard, later Sir Richard Eyre, CBE – soon to be director of the National Theatre – and, as he politely explained to me, he had an arrangement whereby he was permitted to help himself to whatever he fancied, chalk it up and settle at the end of the month. It was the ultimate tab, the true mark of the man's stature.

The catering side of the Playhouse was really humming at this time, largely due to Richard's productions, which ensured full houses – and, as a consequence, a roaring trade

in the bars and restaurants. I had my feet well under the table, and the Playhouse was very much the place to be. As well as the three theatre bars and a hundred-seater restaurant, there was a salad and wine bar - and a public bar too, where people would be standing five deep waiting to get served.

Just a year after I started, in 1975, the theatre received a substantial grant from Nottingham City Council to create a bandstand surrounded by a cobbled and paved area outside the public bar. It was all up and running for the summer of 1976, which turned out to be one of the longest and hottest in British history. And the thirstiest. If ever a young man was in the right place at the right time…

That year we had hundreds drinking on the terrace, night after night. This was great business, and reflected well on me. It seemed we'd created a genuine hot spot in the city. I had to hire extra staff in a hurry, just to get the drinks served. But, like all good things, our success came at a price. Our biggest headache, back in those days of restricted opening hours for pubs, when you could hardly get a drink after ten thirty at night, was how to persuade our customers to leave the premises on time. The law then was that after last orders customers were allowed ten minute's drinking-up time. Simple enough, except that on a Friday and Saturday we might have as many as five hundred people outside. Getting them to finish off their drinks and disperse was a labour of Hercules. The police view was that it was my responsibility, and that if I couldn't do it they might just have to close us down. When I argued that it wasn't on, they replied, 'It's the law.' 'Well then,' I said, quoting Mister Bumble, 'the law is an ass.' It might have got ugly, but in the end the Nottingham Constabulary decided that I genuinely was doing my best and they would turn a blind eye.

As well as all the people drinking outside, we had an after-hours party going on down an alleyway at the side of the theatre. The problem was with the ullage, the waste beer or slops that has to be returned to the brewery for analysis. It was being stored in a dark and dingy alleyway at the side of the building. Such was the volume of business in the bars that we had no space to store any ullage kegs. The problem emerged when the brewery came to fetch it: there was never any left. The reason was the local down-and-outs. They'd discovered where we kept it, and decided it was a crime to let it go to waste. So, night after night, once we'd vacated the premises, they gathered in the alley for a free booze-up. The brewery had no option but to concede. There was nothing to be done about it, and I was able to claim whatever ullage I needed to in order to make my stock control figures add up.

So things were going well for me. I was hob-nobbing with the stars. I counted among my regulars people like Zoe Wannamaker, John Hurt and Mark McManus – who'd recently risen to national fame in the TV series *Sam* and would later be reincarnated as *Taggart*. John and Mark were serious drinkers, and always surrounded by admiring females. I was riding a wave. I had no idea what the future held, and rarely gave it a thought. I was unattached, having split up with Di, I loved my job, and was keeping interesting company.

There's a thin line, of course, between riding a wave and being a cocky little sod. Being in the business I was in, I took risks. We all did. It wasn't easy to get through a night's work without having a drink or two. Customers liked to buy you one, and it felt as though you were doing your duty in accepting. Once the bar was closed, you felt the need to unwind. That meant I sometimes drove home when I shouldn't have done. I was lucky. I didn't do any damage to anybody, and I got out of jail twice by immense good fortune when by rights I should have been booked.

On the first occasion I was driving home to Beeston along the A52 when I realised there was a cop car behind me. There was no reason why he should pull me over, and I was determined not to give him one. I drove nice and steady, and concentrated hard. After a while he seemed to be falling behind me and briefly disappeared from view on a bend. With my turn-off approaching I stamped on the accelerator, aiming to leave the main road before he got me in his sights again. I misjudged it. The perils of driving under the influence, I guess. I found myself slewed across the verge, with the police car pulling up behind me. Out stepped a burly constable, notebook in hand.

I wasn't going to argue. I was in the wrong and I knew it. I just prepared myself for the worst. And then God intervened. Not literally, you understand, but the cop's co-pilot come running up to say there was a serious incident in town and it was 'calling all cars'. The copper put away his notebook and wagged a finger at me. 'You are one lucky young bugger,' he said. 'Next time you won't be. If I ever set eyes on you again, matey, I'm having you.'

I should have learned my lesson, but of course I was young and foolish. And while my good sense occasionally deserted me, my good luck didn't. About a year later I was invited to an after-the-show party with the cast of whatever play was on at the time. I left at four in the morning. The roads were empty, and my head felt pretty clear. What I hadn't taken into account was the fact that there was a major police operation under way. I timed it to perfection, merging onto the main road slap bang in the middle of a substantial convoy of police cars and vans.

They pulled me over. Two senior officers came to the car and told me they wanted to breathalyse me. I played the only card I had. 'It'll have to wait,' I said. 'I just left a party a couple of minutes ago. Literally drained my glass as I left.' They knew what I was talking about, the rule that states you can refuse to be breathalysed until ten minutes after your last drink. I was hoping that the delay to the convoy would be a nuisance, that they'd let me go; but they stood their ground. We would wait ten minutes, during which I smoked non-stop, remembering the advice of a mate, who once told me that nicotine confuses the machine.

Whether that did it or not I'll never know, but the fact is I took the test and got through. And all the way home I kept telling myself, never again, mate, never again.

They were good days at Nottingham. The whole city was buzzing. Not just the theatre, but also the football team. I mean Nottingham Forest who, under the management of Brian Clough, were riding high, winning the League and two consecutive European Cups. Cloughie was one of those characters who was always surrounded by rumours, gossip and half-truths. I was once told a story by someone who claimed to have got it from Archie Gemmell, the diminutive midfield general in that legendary Forest side. Gemmell was negotiating a new contract, and Cloughie told him, 'Archie, you come in here and talk to me as if your were the best player in the world – and if you were a foot taller you would be.'

I had a lot of respect for Clough, mainly because of his achievements as a player and manager. But he also made enemies, my future father-in-law amongst them. Barry was a lifelong supporter of Derby County, the team Clough managed prior to joining Forest. After they won the old First Division title in 1972, Clough was a super-hero in the eyes of Rams supporters. One morning Barry, in suit and tie on his way to the college where he taught, called in at the Baseball Ground to collect tickets for a cup match. As he drove into the car park he realised that Cloughie was pulling in behind him. Barry couldn't believe his luck: here he was face to face with his hero, a footballing god. Grinning from ear to ear he called out, 'Good morning, Mister Clough.' Cloughie looked at him and answered, 'Fuck off.' From that day Barry never attended another Derby game until Clough had departed.

So life was great for me. I had a job I liked, I'd bought a house in Beeston on the proceeds, and I had a company car. It was about to get even better. My area manager, Dennis, asked me to help run a huge catering event in Leicester, and it was there that I met Anne, an A Level student with eyes on a place at York University, where she hoped to study music. By the following autumn, when she moved north to begin her studies, we were very much an item. We both thought York was a fabulous city, and at that time it was still pretty affordable. I'd promised her I'd get out of the licensed trade and look for a job there, otherwise we'd never see each other.

It was while visiting Anne at the University that I ran into Kevin, some years after I'd lost touch with him. We were queuing up for a meal in the college refectory when I happened to look beyond the counter into the kitchen area and spotted a familiar figure. 'I'm sure I know him,' I said, pointing at a bearded figure in a sharp suit. And slowly I realised who it was. I caught his eye; he gave me the hard stare, then realised who I was. We arranged to meet up that night for drinks. Anne brought her best friend with her, a lovely Irish lass called Nikki. It wasn't long before she and Kevin became an item, and later got married. Nikki, a gifted pianist, was typically Irish. I once heard her talking about her dogs. 'Oh,' I asked her, 'how many have you got?' She thought for a moment, then said, 'Four. But two of them's dead.'

Anne was in her final year when we got married down in Leicestershire, at my parent's church in Markfield. Shortly afterwards I was interviewed for the job of Regional Manager for Little Chef, and appointed.

6.
THERE'S MORE TO THIS BREWING LARK THAN I REALISED

After the elation of deciding to partner up, Smithy and I pondered what was quite clear by now: between us we knew very little about brewing. We knew that a lot of it took place in Tadcaster, just down the A64, and we had convinced ourselves that it wasn't too complicated. If you could do it in your own kitchen, why not on an industrial scale?

I'd assumed that, since this was my idea, I would be the brewer. Smithy would distribute it and we'd hire someone to do the selling, someone else to do the books. A four-man team: easy as you like. But how was I going to learn about brewing? Peter Frost, whom I'd met at Lastingham's that first visit, had suggested I talk to a guy called Andrew Whalley.

Andrew, raised in the USA, had settled in Malton some time previously. He played rugby there and, having been made redundant as a design engineer and draughtsman, was languishing at its bacon factory – the Baco. Pigs were not his passion; brewing was, and on his day off he'd come into the

Crown Hotel where a guy called Geoff Woollons was operating the Malton Brewery. Geoff had been in brewing since 1948, mostly at Mitchell & Butlers in Birmingham, so he knew a thing or two, and Andrew would work for nothing, partly to satisfy his passion, partly to learn at the feet of a master. I arranged to meet Andrew at the Tanglewood, out on the Malton road. He impressed me with his enthusiasm, his knowledge and his apparent self-confidence.

I then spoke to Geoff Woollons and asked if I could work a couple of shifts to get some idea of what was involved. 'Certainly,' he said, 'if you show up about four you can watch the process, maybe lend a hand now and then.' 'Oh,' I said, 'four o'clock? I was hoping to put a full day in.' 'You will,' he answered. 'We're talking four in the morning.'

There was a reason for this inhuman regime. It had nothing to do with the brewing process, everything to do with the price of electricity, which was a lot lower in the dead of night. Geoff was in fact very generous, letting us come in like that. For all he knew, we might have stolen all his secrets and set up in opposition, but he was a real ale evangelist. He saw us as potential recruits to a mystical brotherhood – and really, he wasn't far off the mark.

As well as running his own operation, Geoff hosted occasional short brewing courses at the Crown. They were run by a fellow named David Smith. David already had a substantial career behind him, first as a shift brewer, latterly a quality control man for Sam Smith's, and had set himself up as a consultant to people starting micro-breweries. I put my name down for The Fundamentals of Mini Brewing right away. It was a respected course, not just for novices but also for people in the industry. It was a good way of polishing up their practice – and filling in a few gaps in their knowledge. My thinking was that there couldn't be that much to learn and the sooner I got the hang of it the sooner I could start up.

That first day I learned two valuable lessons. One, I couldn't drink. Not with the big boys, anyway. Almost as a matter of course, the crew would gather in the bar of the Crown after a day's work and casually sink six or seven pints. Then it'd be, 'Where we off now?' – i.e., let's go into town and do some serious drinking. I simply wasn't in their league.

David later told me that his whole career had come about as a result of his taste for beer. It was 1976, he'd completed a degree in Chemistry at Essex and was on the point of graduating, when he had a conversation with a tutor. 'He asked me if I had a career in mind,' he said, 'and the fact was I hadn't really given it any serious thought. He asked me what I liked doing. I shrugged my shoulders and said, well, drinking beer. Exams were over and the hottest summer in a generation was in full swing. He suggested I write to the major brewing companies, and that's what I did. The fact that

I'd grown up in York and that Sam Smith's was just down the road – well, when they offered me a job it sort of added up.'

My second lesson was the realisation that I knew absolutely nothing and wasn't going to learn it in a hurry. It was all way too technical. First off, I was baffled by the language they used. I had a vague idea what specific gravity meant, but when we got into microbiology I was lost. Was I really the man to spend days agonising over which yeast to choose – from a list of 400 species stored in deep-freeze at the National Collection of Yeast Cultures in Norwich?

No, I was going to need help. Even I could see that. By the end of my second shift I was ready to go home and re-draft the budget. My project wasn't going to get off the ground unless I hired someone who knew about quality beer – somebody who would be the equivalent of a head chef in a restaurant. And I was pretty sure that man was Andrew Whalley.

The quality of the product is everything. It cannot be compromised...

Meanwhile, Smithy and I tried to gather basic knowledge of this industry we were going to take by storm. We went to Barnsley, home of the South Yorkshire Brewing Company, where David Smith showed us around. Again, he talked a language that was absolutely foreign to our ears. Terms like 'paraflow', 'underback' and 'sparging' had us looking at each other and shrugging our shoulders. What was a conditioning tank? How did you turn the yeast, and why? And why did he keep talking about liquor when we were looking at water?

I remember on the way back David told us how he got interested in micro-brewing. He'd been twelve years at Sam Smith's when the head brewer's position became vacant. 'The guy was retiring after a lifetime with the firm, but he told me the road was blocked for me: they were wanting to bring in new blood. And he suggested that if I wanted to grow I ought to spread my wings.' David looked at opening his own brewery in York, but couldn't see how he could finance it. 'I started offering a consultancy service on the side,' he said, 'and it took off from there. My approach with any new company was that I would be at the steering wheel, and the owners would control the brakes and accelerator.'

David offered to help us find the kit we needed to get started. We crossed the Pennines to look up the defunct Lion brewery in Blackburn, formerly home of Matthew Brown & Co. Their brew kit now lay in bits on the floor of an abandoned furniture factory in Accrington. It had been there since the place closed down. It was like entering a scrap yard – except that it had a roof on it. What I saw was a scattering of round, tarnished steel vessels and a lot of bent and twisted pipes, all surrounded by piles of mouldering sawdust, but David reassured us that it was in good shape. He explained what all the various bits and pieces were, namely, a decent sized twenty-barrel brewery. He said that it was on the large side for a start-up micro-brewery, but that suited us for reasons that would become clear later. More importantly, David pronounced it basically sound, and that night, from home, I made an offer of £19,000. That would account for most of my available capital, so I was hugely relieved when they agreed to hold the price for three months. It was time to put a financial package together – and to find some premises.

Money was going to be a massive issue, so we decided that Smithy should hang onto his job for the time being. One of us needed to be earning while the other one looked around for investors. We needed a fighting fund to get this project off the road. Quite how much was required we didn't yet know; but every time we thought about it the notional sum seemed to grow.

As we totted up what we might need for rental of business premises, plus building works, we shaped our first business plan. That involved a forecast as to our likely progress, and our budgets. What we had in mind was a sum that would fund us to the point where we could produce our first brew, plus a minimum of £10,000 for cash-flow.

First things first, I sold the only asset I had, namely the roof over my head. I got £115,000 for the house in Heslington and paid off two mortgages. That left me with £28,000 in my hand, and nowhere to live. And here's where Kevin stepped into the breach, not for the first time. One of the colleges he looked after had a flat that was kept for visiting academics. It had been ear-marked for a Russian professor who was due to spend a term at York, but he'd pulled out at the last minute, leaving it vacant. Was I interested? I was up there with my deck-chair and my telly before Kevin could change his mind.

Having both worked at a high level for an organisation the size of Little Chef, Smithy and I were well used to bouncing figures around and making improbable forecasts look plausible when presented to a board of directors. We were lucky too to have an ally in the shape of Mal Pickles. Mal and I were team-mates at Heslington cricket club. We'd played in the York Vale league for years. I was a wicket-keeper-batsman, he was a hard-hitting middle-order bat. He knew all about how businesses worked. He ran training courses and had book-keeping skills – invaluable to us in these early days. He would take our rough calculations – crossings-out and all – and re-shape them into a form that a bank manager could understand. More importantly, he made them look as though they were drafted by someone who knew what he was doing.

P*** Up In A Brewery

To raise the rest of the money, I now did what entrepreneurs have always done: I turned to my family, specifically my brother Robin. He'd capitalised on those fabulous A Levels, gained a First in Physics from Newcastle University, and followed up with a PhD. He'd built up his own business in Leeds, Tasman Software Ltd, developing and marketing a word processing program, Tasword, and a range of other business type software for the various microcomputers that had become popular in the 1980s. This was the age of the Sinclair Spectrum, Amstrad CPC and Commodore 64. They were marvels of their time but by 1996 their day was done. So it seemed that I came along at just the right time.

Robin was ready to dissolve his company and said he would be happy to invest in ours. However, as the potential start-up costs escalated, I began to lose heart. When he called one day to ask me how things were going I was at a low point. 'I'm shelving it,' I said. 'We need way more money than I realised.'

'Go on,' he said, 'how much?' I didn't want to tell him, but I took a deep breath and forced it out. 'Sixty grand.' He thought for a minute, then said, 'I can do that. But first I'll send my accountant round to talk you through a few things.'

That talk lasted three hours, during which I took him through the business plan I was working on. He told me he was going to go and look over two or three micro-breweries, and try to get an idea of our likely prospects.

I've always wondered which firms he went to, and what he saw. I never set eyes on the guy again, although a week or two later he did send a report – to Robin, not me. I gather it was quite thick. In fact, Robin never let me see what he wrote. He must have feared it would devastate me. He did, however, talk me through some of the guy's comments.

It wasn't exactly cheering. The meat of it was a long list of reasons why we should not, repeat not, proceed.

Top of the list was that we would face stiff competition in a crowded Yorkshire market-place. A number of small breweries had managed to get a foothold in recent years. There was of course Black Sheep at Masham, Cropton over at the New Inn just outside Pickering, Daleside at Harrogate, Rudgate at Tockwith, and several more. Beyond that was the difficulty of getting access to a market dominated by the big players; and simple, practical things that hadn't occurred to me and Tony, like the fact that pubs took an age to re-cycle your casks, meaning that you needed hundreds and hundreds of them in order to maintain a steady rate of production. Then there was the quality of the beer: it was one thing producing a great brew today, but could you maintain that taste and quality, consistently, time after time, and ensure that the customer always got what he expected? The guy wasn't sure that we'd really worked out the distribution side of things either: how many vans we needed, and drivers. And what about cash-flow? Landlords were notoriously bad payers. Would we be able to make the beer duty payments that were due on the 25th of every month – all except December, when the Revenue got into the spirit of the season and demanded their money on the 24th? Because the Revenue didn't listen to excuses. It was, pay up or we're coming after you. And then, just supposing we did all of the above correctly and got ourselves up and running, were we aware that the big companies would spot a successful start-up and discount their own beer, aggressively, to squeeze us out?

It's hard to listen to that sort of thing and not lose the will to carry on. Looking back, I must have been incredibly resilient – or extremely stupid. However, I learned that there was, at the very end of this damning report, a glimmer of hope. 'If anybody can do it,' the accountant told Robin, 'your brother can.'

As I negotiated all these road-blocks, I clung to one idea which I thought might single us out from the crowd. If I could get what I was after, premises within York's city walls, we would have a unique selling point. We would be 'York's One and Only'. It was a bit like Boddington's, with their highly successful tag-line 'the Cream of Manchester' – except that our beer would be a bloody sight better. From the outset, I was determined that we would be a show brewery. I already had an idea in my mind as to its lay-out, with a balcony around the brew-house and viewing panels from which visitors could observe the process in the fermenting and conditioning rooms. The idea was already taking shape in my head, and was constantly developing. I was also planning a bar and a retail shop which would effectively be a Visitor Centre. So there were two more key points in my thinking. We must have a location within the city walls, one that visitors in York could easily find on foot; and we must create additional sources of revenue.

Somebody needs to be in control… one person must have the final say…

Once we had the makings of a business we had to decide how to allocate the shares. That's more important than people realise. When things are going wrong, somebody needs to be able to say, 'I'm in charge' and that means that somebody needs to have a controlling interest in the enterprise. The plan we came up with was quite simple. This was, in essence, my baby, so I would have 51 per cent. My brother and Smithy, as the other two main investors, would divide the rest, taking 24.5 per cent each. They declared themselves happy with the arrangement, and we all agreed that the new enterprise would be called The York Brewery Company Limited. Smithy and I would be working directors, Robin the sleeping partner and company secretary.

With Robin's money secured, and a further small contribution from a good friend at the cricket club, Brian Milner, we now did the rounds of the banks looking for additional funding. One thing we were starting to learn is that when you can sit down and say, 'Yes, this is how much capital we have' – when you have an absolute ceiling on expenditure – it doesn't half concentrate the mind on budgeting. It also makes you a tougher negotiator. You are constantly aware of where your boundaries are. Smithy and I had written a business plan, on the basis of which we were ready to approach the banks for financing.

We filled it with the kind of jargon beloved of bankers: managing cash-flow, maximising profits, assuring no overall over-spend on variable expenditure. We made sure that our projected cash flow never got anywhere near the red zone in that crucial first year – and that it rocketed off the top of the page in year three. We didn't believe a word of what we put down, but that wasn't the point. The point was to get the bank on our side. Without them the whole thing was dead in the water.

Smithy and I spent days drafting a well-informed, humorous, credible and realistic view of a business that would offer any bank a gilt-edged opportunity to make money, year after year. We rehearsed our spiel over and over, then did the rounds, delivering a polished performance to one banking house after another. Barclays, Lloyds, Yorkshire and the Halifax were united in their response. It was indeed a humorous and slick presentation which they thoroughly enjoyed, but... good to meet you, and if you can show yourselves out, thank you. It was only at the fifth time of asking, at NatWest, that we met a manager, Stuart Wilson, who understood us and shared our vision. He agreed to loan us £30,000, to make a further £10,000 available for cash flow, and to throw in free banking for the first twelve months.

Armed with a bank account and a company cheque-book, we went to a firm of accountants recommended by Stuart. Clive Owen and Co had only recently opened a York office, managed by a lovely fellow named Terry Doyle who would prove invaluable over the coming years. For the record, our back-of-a-fag-packet calculations at this stage were as below:

Monies IN		Monies OUT	
Tony Thomson shares, 51 per cent	£25,500	Brew plant	£19,000
Tony Smith shares 24.5 per cent	£12,250	Fabrication of brew plant	£15,000
Robin Thomson shares 24.5 per cent	£12,250	6 x conditioning tanks	£7,000
Tony Thomson, Director's loan	£19,000	2 x fermenting vessels	£8,000
Tony Smith, Director's loan	£9,000	Building works	£60,000
Robin Thomson, Director's loan	£48,000	Decoration	£10,000
Bank loan	£30,000	Boiler	£12,000
		Legals	£3,000
		Architect	£3,000
		Brewing materials	£5,000
		Van	£5,000
		Sundry opening costs	£5,000
Total	**£156,000**	**Total**	**£152,000**

We knew that those figures wouldn't sustain us, as Stuart kept warning us. Cash flow is key, and even with the £10,000 overdraft facility we were plainly sailing too close to the wind.

On Stuart's advice I managed to ease the pressure a little by approaching Lombard, the commercial arm of NatWest bank, and agreeing a 'lease to buy' deal on the additional kit we needed to supplement the brew plant we'd bought in Blackburn – six conditioning tanks, two new 20-barrel fermenters and a boiler. For around £550 a month over five years the equipment would be ours. While that added to our monthly liabilities it freed up some £30,000 for cash flow – something for which we were going to be hugely grateful in the months ahead.

Stuart kept ramming home the point about cash flow being the lifeblood of a business, especially one like ours. He reminded us that 60 per cent of new businesses that failed within their first three years did so because they 'over-traded' or simply expanded too fast and ran out of cash. Only 40 per cent went under through lack of sales. For firms with cash-flow issues, there simply comes a time when the bank turns off the tap.

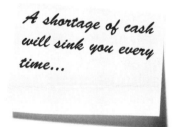

A shortage of cash will sink you every time...

7.
LOOKING FOR A HOME

So now we had a plan, we had the finance, and we had much of the kit we required to start brewing. It seemed it was time to find a place to call home.

We'd been looking, of course, but a city like York isn't exactly bursting with empty buildings at knock-down prices. And our needs were special. We needed something pretty sizeable. We needed it to be affordable, and we needed it to be inside the city walls. We also needed to be not too close to any residential areas, because, as any visitor to Tadcaster or Burton-on-Trent will tell you, brewing is a smelly business – and not everybody loves that particular fragrance.

As for location, that was one area where I wasn't going to compromise at any price. It was clear to me that if the brewery relied 100 per cent on beer sales it would be vulnerable to all sorts of unpredictable factors – like the weather, the state of the economy, and the fortunes of the England football team. I felt it was crucial that we develop other sources of income. As a major tourist centre, York is host to seven million visitors a year, most of whom trail around the city on foot. Why not put on brewery tours? Why not incorporate a bar and catering facilities, making it a place people would want to visit?

So I enquired of all the commercial estate agents in town, and walked the streets till my feet ached. Just my luck that I set out on that particular quest in one of the hottest Augusts on record. I soon had blistered heels, and went in search of more suitable footwear. I felt a right pillock stomping through the hordes of visitors in my T-shirt, shorts and size nine hiking boots, but I comforted myself with the thought that this time next year I'd be selling these people the first local beer York had produced in forty years.

I don't know how many miles I covered. York's not a big city, but it has a lot of hot, narrow streets. It seemed that every time I came across a vacant property with commercial potential it was either too big or too small, too expensive or slap bang next to a row of houses whose residents would raise objections. There were plenty of likely sites on the outskirts of town – sites that were cheap and offered room for expansion – but how many visitors are going to get a bus out to the by-pass for a brewery tour?

Stick to your plan. Don't take easy options...

Three weeks into our search, the only good news was that I'd broken in my new walking boots and lost eight pounds. And then I got a call from David Waterhouse at Waterhouse & Robinson. 'I've taken on a property on Toft Green,' he said. 'Could be just what you're looking for.'

P*** Up In A Brewery

Toft Green is a back-street sandwiched between Micklegate and the railway offices at George Hudson House. It's inside the Bar Walls – in fact, almost overshadowed by them. Smithy and I visited the premises and made an initial assessment. It was old, dirty and dilapidated. Smithy's reaction as we stumbled around in the gloom and dust spoke for both us. 'How can anyone let a building get into this sodding state?' he said. 'Tossers.' The ground floor hadn't been used in five years, since the motorcycle dealer packed up and left. The upper floor, which had been vacant twelve years, had previously been a carpet warehouse for the furniture store Whitby C Oliver. They had leased off the whole building to Bright Reasons Restaurants Ltd, one of whose companies, Pizzaland, currently occupied the part that fronted onto Micklegate. Smithy spent most of that first visit prowling around, poking the brickwork and beams and muttering, 'What's holding the bloody place up anyway?'

Unattractive it certainly was, but we could have no complaints about the size. This was a sprawling jumble of rooms and work-spaces. Upstairs was a whole suite of rooms fronting onto Micklegate which had been sub-let to some Government project that helped re-habilitate drug users. What David was offering us was perhaps a tenth of the entire premises. Parts of it were boarded up, and much of the original structure was covered over with cheap cladding of one kind or another. I wanted to know what was underneath all the chipboard and hardboard: if the place was to have potential as a tourist attraction it needed to be easy on the eye. We returned for a second visit, this time armed with a pick-axe and a sledge-hammer, and set about seeing what the place was made of.

Upstairs we ripped off the plaster-boarding and exposed a real treasure: a super set of king-span beams supporting an octagonal raised roof. It was what you'd call a feature, a real eye-catcher. Perfect for a bar area.

Buoyed up by this find, I called a meeting. Andrew Whalley, the man I'd pencilled in as our probable head brewer, David Smith, the man who would guide us through the process of getting started, and Smithy. Andrew and David's initial concerns were, very sensibly, practical ones. Would the brew kit, still awaiting collection, fit inside the Toft Green site? The mash tun, the copper, the hot and cold liquor tanks and so on – these are large bits of equipment. Was there space for a fermenting room, which had to be kept nice and warm, and a separate conditioning room, which had to be kept cool? Ours was a twenty-barrel brew plant, a barrel being equivalent to thirty-six gallons. Every brew would produce 5,760 pints – which had to be stored prior to delivery. This wasn't a back-kitchen start-up; it was a fair-sized operation.

A twenty-barrel plant was in fact way more than we would have needed to kick-start the business, but we were looking ahead to the medium-term future. With a large plant we wouldn't have to brew so often. That meant we ought to be able to get by with a skeleton staff. Secondly, we wanted our operation to look substantial to the hordes of visitors we were confidently expecting to welcome once the doors were open. Thirdly, in the long-term this place could save us money. As we expanded our distribution network we wouldn't need to upgrade to a bigger plant.

Smithy and I hadn't a clue about whether or not the kit would fit. We left Andrew and David to do the sums in their heads. We lit up our fags – yes, we both smoked in those far-off days: it eased the stress – and poked our heads upstairs, exploring these miscellaneous extra rooms. It was a little rabbit-warren, with moulded panelled doors, low ceilings and narrow stairways with ornate balustrades. We knew we'd need an office or two, but we were also planning that elevated viewing gallery from which visitors could get a good view of the brewing process and not get under the feet of the staff or create health and safety issues. The question was, how would our landlords feel about us carving out half the floor-space to accommodate a gallery on the first floor that would overlook the brew-house below?

We also needed a grain store, which had to be dry and, preferably, close by the grist case, so that we didn't waste man-hours – and energy – humping sacks across from one place to the other. As Smithy and I discussed all these factors and the other two paced up and down, measuring and taking notes, we were able to persuade ourselves that we were getting the hang of this brewery lark. We actually believed that we knew what we were talking about. And we got a real boost when the other two concluded that the interior ought to accommodate the brew kit – so long as we were very careful.

Take into account plans for growth... can you expand in these premises?

At this stage we were still desperately worried about the money situation – and here I made a major breakthrough, negotiating the rent down from an initial £9,000 a year to £4,500 for the first two years, this on the basis that we were having to do so much building and decorating work to get the place in order. The deal was made with Oliver's sub-tenants; we now had to obtain the permission of the superior landlords - that is, of the building's owners, Whitby C Oliver Ltd.

I arranged a meeting with Mr Donald Oliver, and found

him to be a real gentleman, one of the old school. He was in his eighties, and as we toured the building he told me some of its history. The business was started in 1897 by his father, formerly apprentice to a cabinet-maker and upholsterer on Coney Street, John Taylor. The original premises fronted Micklegate but reached all the way back to Toft Green and at various times housed a French polishing establishment, a cabinet maker's, an undertaker's and, latterly, a furniture store. The Micklegate premises, he explained, were much older than the Toft Green buildings and had at least one claim to fame, being the birthplace of Joseph Hansom, inventor of the Hansom cab. Appropriately enough, the area which we would later turn into a bar was, he told me, the very spot where he used to treat customers to a glass of sherry while they viewed carpets.

Donald Oliver and I parted on good terms. He said he was happy to approve our plans – even if they did mean that we would knock a huge hole in the floor to accommodate the brew-house gallery. With his blessing secured, we were now able to proceed with the planning application.

This was a procedure quite new to me. Our application was heard in an open meeting at the Guildhall in York, quite a grand setting, and a potentially intimidating one. We were in a large room set out rather like a theatre. The Planning Committee, consisting of fourteen Councillors, were seated on a stage behind a row of microphones. After awaiting my turn in the public seating I was asked to stand and put my case. I had two minutes in which to tell them why I thought they ought to approve. Not a lot of time, but I'd prepared thoroughly. I have no idea how I performed, but I do remember that when I sat down afterwards the guy behind me prodded me in the back and said, 'Good luck to you, lad. It's about time we had a decent local beer in this city.'

The Chairman asked whether anybody would like to speak against my plan. I remember waiting, shoulders hunched, holding my breath, bracing myself for the opposition to open fire. There was no response at all. Nothing. He then read out two written objections that had come in from people living near our premises, expressing concern about noise and smells. There followed an open debate about the pros and cons. I was itching to get involved and add my two-pennies' worth, but I'd had my moment. The debate didn't last long, and we moved swiftly to the vote.

I could hardly believe what I heard. There was one abstention, one vote against, and twelve in approval. We were through. For this I had to thank the Police Licensing Officer, Arthur Swain. He had gone on record as being happy for the application to proceed, so long as we weren't licensed to sell liquor. Micklegate has plenty of pubs, and a notorious 'run', for which people – young men, mostly – get a pint or two at every establishment from the Bar walls down to the bottom of the hill where it joins Rougier Street, where they either collapse or start fighting. It's an honourable York tradition, but in Arthur's opinion we didn't need any more boozers, and the planners agreed. I liked Arthur. He was a proper beer man. After he retired he took over the Falcon on Micklegate.

It was now time to find legal representation. I'd recently completed divorce proceedings with Anne, and was very pleased with the way my solicitor, a fellow called Mark Hepworth, handled the whole business. He'd managed to bring a bit of humour to a legal procedure not generally known for its comedy moments. Naturally, I went to his firm, Denison Till, to hunt up a representative for the new venture. The guy I got was good at his job, but his idea of attending to detail meant that he did everything by the book. Every time. Every inch of the way. He made a slow and dull business seem excessively dreary. When I told my man that, whether or not the lease had been signed, I intended to start the building work on April 1st 1996 – perhaps not the most auspicious date in the calendar – he was appalled. 'Tony,' he said, 'you can't do it. You just can't. The lease isn't completed yet.'

I told him he'd had enough time to get all that sorted. 'I can't wait any longer,' I said. 'The builders are coming in on Monday. I've booked them. Too late to stop them, I'm afraid.'

His reply was that he was going on holiday that day and we should wait until he returned. 'Well, you have a great time,' I said. 'I'm going to set these men to work.' 'But how can I enjoy my holiday when I know they'll be serving an injunction on you the minute you get started?' 'Don't worry,' I said, 'I'll deal with it.'

He wasn't happy, at all. His final words were, 'Well, I wash my hands of the whole thing.' He went on his hols on Saturday, and on Monday the builders moved in.

Regency Home and Design were a Doncaster firm. They'd done a lot of work for me in my Little Chef days. I rated them highly, and they appreciated the numerous contracts I'd sent their way, so they were keen to do a good job. Obviously I wanted them to do it right, but I also wanted them to crack on. Sensibly or not, I'd set myself a target: to raise a glass of our own beer within twelve months of the day I was unceremoniously booted out of Little Chef. That was in June 1995, which meant that we needed to be brewing by mid-May.

So we had a target: six weeks to transform a ramshackle set of buildings into a fully functioning, twenty-barrel brewery. The builders sent in ten lads, and they worked ten hours a day, six days a week, right the way through. Heroes, every one of them.

While we blithely carried on with the improvements, I thought it would be a smart move to tell our landlords what was going on, before they heard it from other sources. I broke the news in the form of an invitation to their estate manager, a Mr Bumstead. 'Come down and see what we're doing,' I said. 'I think you'll be pleased.' He came, he saw and he concurred. 'Only one problem,' he added. 'The lease hasn't been signed. You shouldn't be in here.' He followed up by threatening us with an injunction. I suspect he felt it was his duty to do so, but he soon relaxed and made it plain it wasn't high on his list of priorities, and he would get the lease signed as soon as Mr Happy returned from his holidays.

8.
COULD YOU ORGANISE
A PISS-UP IN A BREWERY?

Smithy had timed his notice at Little Chef to run out just as the builders moved in. He said goodbye to a decent salary and a company car, put his best suit in the wardrobe, donned a pair of old jeans, a woolly sweater and a set of thermals – that building was like a refrigerator first thing in the morning – and joined me for a new, if temporary, career as a builder's labourer.

Smithy was in some ways a lucky fellow. He had a huge extended family in Leeds, and they believed in looking out for each other. Later, he would recruit a whole tribe of cousins, nephews and nieces when it was all hands on deck.

Right now, though, it was money he needed. He'd really dived into the project head-first. He'd sold his house, moved in with his mother, and now he borrowed ten grand off his sister, Angie, which he invested in the new company. Little Chef had given him a modest pay-out, and that too went into the York Brewery account. Talk about putting your money where your mouth is. While the builders set about knocking seven shades of shit out of the ground floor walls, Smithy and I tackled the floors upstairs with an industrial sander. The big old solid boards would come up beautifully. I donned a face-mask and goggles. Smithy found his own way of dealing with the dust: he lit up a fag, and as soon as that went out he lit another one. I was still smoking at that time, so I wasn't able to pin the blame entirely on him when we came in one morning and found the lads standing around a hole in the floor, up on the gallery we were building. The hole was ringed with charred wood, smouldering. We had been last to leave the previous night, so we had to accept the blame. Still, the place hadn't burned down. We whispered a prayer of thanks, left them to repair it, and carried on.

As well as sanding the floors, we went along all the many beams we'd exposed, yanking out lengths of half perished cables and removing the nails and clips that had held them in place. As we worked we swept the floors and mopped up for the builders, filling skip after skip with rubble and other rubbish. Before we went home we made sure we dotted buckets around the place to catch the drips.

The roof had leaked from the start – but only when it rained – and it would be some time before we could afford to fix it properly. So each night we were stiff and aching, and each morning we returned nursing pains in muscles we never knew we had, our hands patched with sticking-plasters. In those few weeks I got through three pairs of old jeans and two pairs of leather gloves. Sundays, when the builders took the day off, we went in and cleaned up after them, washing paint off the walls with high-pressure hoses. And when we had nothing better to do we'd sit there with a cigarette and a cup of tea and ask ourselves the question for the umpteenth time. Why in God's name had we got into this?

As the upper floor took shape we turned our attention to the downstairs floor, a mixture of old wooden boards, crazed quarry-tiles, broken bricks and cracked concrete. It had to be strengthened to take the massive weight of the vessels – massive when filled with liquor, that is. They also needed to incorporate a drainage system to cope with the daily hosing down. The only solution was to lay the drains, concrete over the lot, then seal it with a water-proofing resin.

By the end of April we were ready to bring in the brew kit, and to put our head brewer, Andrew Whalley, on full-time hours. His first job was to supervise the introduction and positioning of the various vessels – although before he could do that there was the small matter of fetching them over from across the Pennines. We brought them on a low-loader, which Smithy and I followed, hard up against its tail-lights, every mile of the way. You go through a lot of emotions, watching £19,000-worth of newly-acquired plant crawling along the M62 with the rain sweeping across on a gale-force wind. You feel a certain pride, a shiver of fear and a lot of anxiety. What if it crashes? What if it gets blown off? What if it falls apart? What if it doesn't work – or doesn't fit?

We took our precious cargo to Hull, where a local firm called H&M (Henry and Mike) re-fabricated and re-furbished it. The mash-tuns had giant electric elements to heat the water. Gas was a much cheaper option, so we converted them to an 'indirect' system using steam delivered in copper pipes from a gas boiler. That, and the purchase of a boiler, set us back about £24,000, but it was well worth it in the long run. As David still loves to point out, the savings in power bills over the years paid for that outlay several times over.

Once the work was done it was back on the low-loader and along the A1079. There was a surreal moment when our precious cargo growled past the Little Chef at Shiptonthorpe.

We thought for a moment that the driver was going to pull in for a coffee, but mercifully he drove on. As well as the Lion kit there were six conditioning tanks from a dairy which had to be adapted to the demands of the brewing process.

Andrew was there when we showed up at Toft Green, chewing his nails. He wasn't entirely sure at this stage how we were going to get each part inside the premises. At the very least it was going to be a tight squeeze. And then there was the job of ensuring each item was correctly positioned on the ground floor. It came down to some very precise measurements. According to his calculations there would be as little as half an inch of clearance beside the dividing walls in some cases – not that the walls were built yet: we weren't going to lay a single brick until he'd got every item in position. But first, the problem of getting the kit inside.

Every piece – and most of it was large, heavy and awkward – had somehow to be manoeuvred in through spaces that never really looked wide enough or high enough. But they were – just. In most cases the item was lifted off the delivery lorry by crane and persuaded through the front of the building, on Toft Green, through what had once been the shop window and was now a great gaping hole surrounded by dusty jags of nineteenth-century brickwork. Using the combined muscle of ten builders, plus a little assistance from the Board of Directors – namely, Smithy and me – we slowly worked each vessel onto the precise spot marked out on the plans, and lowered it onto the newly laid concrete floor. Of course we had to get the order right. There was no room for juggling inside the building. First came the conditioning tanks. Once they were in position a wall was put up to complete the conditioning room, where the brewed beer would be cooled and kept at around 11 degrees C (52 F) until it was ready to go into casks. Four twenty-barrel fermenters followed – two of them brand new, two of them re-fabricated – and another wall went up.

The actual brew-house, which was to be at the front of the building facing Toft Green, comprised the mash tun, the underback, the copper, the hot liquor tank and cold liquor tank – 'liquor' in brewing parlance simply meaning treated water. In addition there were the paraflow and a number of hoses and valves, plus steam and various other pipes connecting the vessels to each other. For some reason – Sod's Law, I suppose – most of these were either at ankle height, perfect for tripping you up, or a few feet higher, just right for decapitating the unwary operative. But, as Smithy pointed out, it's amazing how fast you learn when you've gone through the pain barrier six times in a single shift.

The copper vessel, in which the hops were added to the boiling wort, was in fact no such thing. It was made of galvanised steel. However, this was going to be a show brewery and I wanted a bit of 'show', so we had the fabrication guys clad it in a copper skin which we would thereafter have to polish weekly. It was a pain in the neck, but the visitors – when they finally showed up – loved it. It looked authentic. I was gung-ho for adding a wooden outer to the mash tun, but was shot down by Smithy who, as I may have mentioned, was very Yorkshire with money.

There was a minor hiccup when Andrew confessed to having piped up the paraflow, or heat exchanger, backwards. This is the system whereby coppered wort at 90 degrees C is cooled to 20 before it enters the fermenter. Not a major disaster, but it made some of us go hot and cold all over, rather as it would the liquor – and everyone was a lot happier when calm was restored.

Still with our visitors in mind, we now had to lash out a pile of money on shatter-proof glass at the viewing stations we were installing along the walkway that overlooked the fermenting and conditioning rooms. The last thing we wanted was some poor tourist falling into the fermenter. It would doubtless taint the beer.

All during this process, David had been taking a keen interest in the buildings we occupied. Like me, he was intrigued by the king-span beams above what was to be the bar area. After inspecting them for some time he came up with the theory that the place must have been a maltings at some stage. The king-span, he reckoned, was designed to accommodate the particular type of kiln in which the grain used to be roasted.

Despite the difficulties we'd had in getting the brew kit in, we now found, to our delight, that we had some spare space below the area that was to be the visitors' bar. We measured it carefully and calculated that there was room for a stillage area housing ten casks – plus a few kegs for our lager-supping friends. It was always our intention to serve a range of decent lagers in the bar. This discovery got my creative juices flowing as I thought about the hospitality side of the business. I was already drafting flyers and posters with the tag-line, 'Could you organise a piss-up in a brewery?'

As the builders finished off the interior walls, Smithy and I started thinking about the jobs we'd designated for each other. My role would be to run the Visitor Centre and drum up sales, while Smithy took charge of the deliveries. We soon realised there would be a pile of paperwork, which neither of us fancied. We knew we needed help, and went out to find a part-time secretary. What we were after was someone who could type up and send out all our sales literature, someone who would be familiar with the jargon and be prepared to get on the phone and sell our beer. He or she had to be ready to go from the first week in May, based on the assumption that we would meet my end-of-May deadline for selling that first brew.

Our first recruit was a lovely young girl – willing, punctual and polite – but we soon realised she just wasn't up to it. Smithy and I had a chat, wished her well, paid her up and parted company.

One morning while I was pondering where to find a replacement a large boiler came lumbering up Toft Green on the back of a flat-bed truck. It was, of course, second-hand, and it had cost us £12,000. To Smithy and me it looked very heavy, very complicated, very scary and nowhere near as shiny as we'd hoped. The company we'd bought it from, Doncaster Boilers Ltd, unloaded it, positioned it, ran a few tests and pronounced it ready to go. With me as his labourer, Andrew piped it up to the power and water supplies. Slowly the thing came to life, hissing, gurgling, rattling and generally sounding irritable as plumes of steam leaked out from its joints.

A small company can't carry people who aren't fit for the task...

...stick to the terms of contract, but act immediately to save time and money

Old, crotchety and noisy it may have been but this beast was a crucial component of the plant, its very heart-beat. It would not only provide the heat for the sparging arm of the mash tun, for boiling up the copper and heating up the hot liquor tank, but also for cask-washing, and of course hot water for washing glasses in the bar area. Sadly it didn't provide a heating system for the building. There was no such thing, just a few calor-gas heaters scattered here and there,

which were about as much use as a collection of chocolate tea-pots.

With the plant all in position, Andrew turned on the water supply. It immediately started spurting from a dozen or more weak spots, flooding the floor and driving us into the street. That put the drips from the roof into perspective. The most spectacular leaks were sending plumes of water fifteen and twenty feet high, drenching the viewing galleries. Streams flowed across the floor and down the drains. Well, someone said, at least they're working. The noise, in a shell of a building filled with metal containers, was astounding. It was as if we'd stumbled onto a set for filming *Titanic*.

Throughout this Andrew and his team of plumbers kept admirably cool. This was par for the course, they said, as they splashed back and forth with pipe-wrenches, tightening all the valves, and getting to work with the blow-lamps. They soon had everything more or less water-tight. After the noise and confusion of the initial test, we reckoned we could cope with the odd drip here and there.

Looking around at the newly installed vessels, we noticed that the ground floor suddenly seemed cramped. We wondered whether we would have room for everything, notably for racking the beer in casks – plus all the empties we would need to have in readiness. I'd been aware all along that there was a set of store-rooms to one side of the passageway that led into the building – to the right side, to be precise, and strictly speaking beyond the bounds of the part we'd rented. They were crammed full of rubbish. I mean actual trash in plastic sacks and damp cardboard boxes. Every time I walked past them I found myself thinking how useful the extra space would be. I started to crave it, at the same time well aware that we had no money to rent more space.

There's nothing like being skint to prompt a bit of direct action. I collared Smithy and together we dragged all the crap out of the store-rooms. There were six in all, more like old-fashioned coal sheds. Once they were empty we put locks on the doors. They proved to be worth their weight in gold to us, and the best of it was our landlords never seemed to notice what we'd done. Either that or they didn't really care.

While all this was going on our solicitor had returned from Spain in a happier frame of mind. He got together with Mr Bumstead and sorted out the lease, as previously negotiated. £9,000 a year but only half that for the first two years. These were exciting days – tense, yes, but lots happening. The building work was on course for completion to deadline, and the plan was to put our first brew through on the 17th of May. It looked as though I'd be raising that celebratory first pint on June 1st, as planned.

Just in time, we hired a new our part-time secretary. Joanne was straight in at the deep end, her first job being to get the sales packs ready and prepare to flood the market-place – namely, every pub in the York area. The packs contained a letter on our super headed paper explaining who we were and how delighted we were to be able to offer the York pubs a locally brewed beer for the first time in forty years. We enclosed white plastic pump clips for each of our first two brews, Yorkshire Terrier and Stonewall. We enclosed too a brief description of our brewery, highlighting the fact that our beer contained no added preservatives and stressing that all the ingredients were natural and healthy. Finally, we baited the hook.

Like many a business before us, we'd had a long think and come up with a once-in-a-lifetime offer. Buy One Get One Free. It was divinely simple, and could not fail – could it? Order a nine-gallon cask of ale and we'll give you a second for nothing. You want eighteen gallons? Same thing. No problemo. Now, who in their right mind would turn down an offer like that? We told Joanne to brace herself for the massive orders that would doubtless come flooding in.

Having set Joanne to work, we decided we really ought to find her an office. We didn't have one yet, just a couple of dusty rooms – and certainly nothing with which to furnish them. However, I had an idea where I might, with a bit of luck, find what we needed.

When I was given the heave-ho from Little Chef the regional office for the north-east was closed down too. That was at Barnsdale Bar South, on the A1 between Doncaster and Pontefract. I picked up the phone and called my old mate John Collins, who had been my neighbouring Regional Director in the Midlands and was now overseeing my old patch. 'Now then,' I said, 'any idea what happened to all the gear in my office?'

He thought for a moment, then said, 'It'll be where you left it, all locked up and left to rot. Nobody's been in there as far as I know.' 'Oh, 'cos I'm looking for one or two bits and pieces – you know, desk, chair, that kind of thing. Any chance that I could... ' 'Yeah, sure, go ahead. But we'll have to show a sale for the paperwork, like.' 'How about a hundred quid?' I asked. 'Would that do?' 'I should think so. Just help yourself to what you need.'

When I picked Smithy up for the drive down there I was at the wheel of the biggest van Enterprise would hire me. Smithy looked inside it and said, 'Bloody hell, Tony, I thought we were getting a few bits and pieces.' 'Yeah,' I said, 'we are. Just wanted to make sure we had plenty of room.'

It was a Sunday, and there was no chance of any of Little Chef's senior management being out and about. By the time we drove home that afternoon the van was literally groaning. I can't recall the full inventory, but top of the list was my old Regional Director's desk, and my fancy leather Regional Director's chair, with adjustable seat and castors. Both items have been in my study ever since and have kept me comfortable throughout the process of writing this book. There were other bits and pieces, including a number of desks, a couple of tables, a whole pile of chairs; there were filing cabinets, desk lamps, book shelves, computer tables, even fridges – handy for storing our yeast – and a whole range of smaller items: trays, desk files, desk mats, and fans.

They say revenge is a dish best served cold. I'm not sure this was revenge, but I did feel as though I'd compensated myself for the way they fired me. We now had a pair of lavishly equipped offices. Into the larger one – which wasn't large at all – we managed to squeeze four desks: one for Joanne, one for me, another for Smithy, and a fourth for whoever we could persuade to come and do our books. The other, even more cramped office, we generously donated to Andrew. As Head Brewer, he surely deserved it.

9.
SORRY, WE ARE *NOT* CALLING IT 'THE DOG'S BOLLOCKS'

Having taken on Joanne, of course, we had to pay her out of our sparse resources. I was aware that there were various schemes to give start-up businesses a helping hand, and began looking around. We were delighted to come across a statutory grant worth £1,000 towards the salary of any new full-time employee who was kept on for a minimum of six months. That didn't include Joanne, but three of us did meet the criteria – namely, myself, Smithy and Andrew. That meant we could claim £3,000. It all helped.

We then heard of a Government scheme that gave money to firms employing anyone who had been out of work for six months. They would pay their wages for three months – and there was no compulsion on either side to extend their contract. This was too good to miss. I went to meet the man who ran the scheme in York, a chap called Andrew Wragg. I already knew Wraggy as a fellow member of the Wanderers cricket club, the Sunday side I had occasionally played for.

They didn't have a home ground and always played away, hence their name. Their fixtures were carefully arranged. They had to be at decent clubs – and they had to have a proper bar.

Wraggy was deeply committed to the scheme he ran, and a big supporter of the people he recruited to it. We were approaching the date when we would need someone, and hugely attracted by the idea of not paying whoever it was for the first three months. Both Smithy and I agreed it was perfect for us. It's easy to hire people who seem okay at first but ultimately prove unsuitable. This three-month window would give us a chance to evaluate any new recruit.

Before I went to Wraggy I had to think about the kind of person who might suit our needs. It was the beginning of May and we were fast approaching our deadline. We needed every part of the operation to be ready to go, and that meant lining up a nice row of squeaky clean casks in which to rack the beer. The team had managed get the cask wash ready for operation. We just needed an operator. I'd paid little attention to this part of the business. We were here to brew beer. Cask-washing sounded simple. The way I imagined it, the casks came in from the pubs and bars empty. You'd roll them out on a conveyor belt, press a button and they'd roll off the other end a few minutes later all bright, shiny and clean.

I could not have been more wrong – at least, as far as a modest little start-up affair like ours was concerned. For the big brewers there was indeed a simple, automated system available. However, to buy that kind of plant would have cost us as much as we'd spent on the entire project all over again. No, it might be a bit Heath Robinson, but we would do things the old-fashioned way. It began with Andrew sitting me down, making sure I was concentrating, then spelling it out. 'Nobody is going to be let loose on the cask-cleaning job until they've learned what I'm about to teach you. Every last word of it.' He paused, and waited for me to say yes. 'Yes,' I said. 'Fire away.' I had no idea what I was in for. How hard is it to wash out a few old casks? 'Right,' he said, 'there is a process, and you have to adhere to it in every last detail every time you clean a cask. Okay?' 'Okay,' I said.

'Any cask coming in here could have all kinds of evil bugs lurking in its insides. So it has to be sterilised – thoroughly – after every use. We cannot afford to run the slightest risk of an infection getting into the beer. There are no short-cuts. Think of what's at risk,' he said. But before I had the chance to do that he was up and running. 'We've got a hundred bags of brewer's malted barley, right?' I nodded. I was still aching from hauling the 25 kilo bags up two flights of stairs and into the grain store, still wincing every time I thought about the dent they made in our cash resources – and a further dent some weeks later when we yielded to the inevitable and installed a mechanical hoist. Our malted barley came from Fawcetts of Castleford, owned and managed by the passionate James Fawcett, a grandson of the founder. James had had his fingers burned a few times over the years by breweries that never quite made it, and would only accept cash in those early months.

I cast aside such concerns and let Andrew hammer home his point. 'And we load twenty of them into the grist case, yes?' Who could forget humping them up to that large wooden box on the balcony, from where the contents would be fed into the mash tun? 'And then,' Andrew continued, 'then there's all the money we lashed out on those 'pockets' of hops.' Those too we'd dragged up by hand – also to the grain store; although to be fair, they did smell nice. 'So,' he said, 'if, after all that expenditure of sweat, energy and money, and then the ten days of fermenting, cooling and conditioning, some ignorant twat – be he a minion on a Government scheme or the Managing Director himself – if said twat allowed the precious beer to be racked into casks which he had failed to purge of all its nasty little bacteria….' Andrew paused, and I braced myself. 'If he did that, and if I took that pick-axe' – he was looking at the big ugly tool I'd been using to extract the keystones from the dirty casks – 'and rammed it up his jacksey so hard he'd still be limping when he drew his frigging pension – would you blame me?'

I had to agree that a guy would be perfectly justified in losing his composure, and promised him I would do precisely what he was about to tell me to. Because this was just the preamble to a very long lecture about a very lengthy procedure. It was all a part of my education, of course; and, once Andrew had supervised the entire ball-aching, sweaty, repetitive and noisy routine, I was able to draft a job description for Wraggy. Whoever we got needed to be fit, strong and able to carry out mind-numbingly dull tasks without cutting corners. Rather than label the job honestly – 'Wanted: Human Donkey' – I craftily dressed it up as 'Cask Washer and Beer Racker', then hurried off to see Wraggy.

By now I had two positions to fill. In the sales office, Joanna already had her hands full, so Smithy was looking for someone to set up a computer programme we could all manage, and generally look after the books and run the office. We realised this was a full-time position. We imagined an ageing, craggy Yorkshireman who understood our need to be frugal – and of course it would help if he liked beer. In between drawing up job descriptions, Smithy and I would sit down and check through our lists. Yes, we were still making lists – every day of the week – and calling regular meetings.

After our daily meeting, it was back to the heat and squalor of the cask-washing – with the occasional break to chase Wraggy and ask when he was going to send me someone. As I sorted through the jumbled pile of dirty casks I cast my mind back to all the times I'd watched draymen handling full ones with style and ease. They made it look like a sort of dance routine, a thing of grace and beauty. I was handling empties, and blundering my way through it with a total lack of co-ordination. Still, I never was much of a dancer. I went at it with a will. This was my baby – admittedly, more the nappy-changing end of things rather than the bedtime stories – and I was determined to show myself capable of performing any task that was thrown at me. I took care to bend at the knees, to wear my protective gloves – and of course I always, always, had on my steel toe-capped boots. Even an empty cask, dropped on an unprotected foot, could be cripplingly painful.

At the start-up stage, arrange regular meetings...

Just when I thought I could take no more, Wraggy phoned to say he'd pulled a rabbit out of the hat. Next day a young, confident, fit-looking lad called Steve joined our happy band of brothers. He got stuck in as if he was a man on a mission – and he probably was: namely, to secure a job. He certainly impressed us all. I asked Andrew to run through the training spiel he'd given me – but maybe to leave out the bit about the pick-axe.

Wraggy had also found someone who, he thought, might suit the role of office manager and book-keeper. He had in fact unearthed the guy we'd dreamed of, a craggy old Yorkshireman who had a lifetime's experience of watching the cash-flow – i.e., counting pennies – and who confessed to a passion for cask ale. We hired Roy Heseltine before he had a chance to find out what he was getting into.

Sorry, We Are *Not* Calling It 'The Dog's Bollocks'

My own personal D-day – one year since my dismissal from Little Chef, and the date I'd set for sinking that first delicious pint – was fast approaching. We now parted company with our friends the builders. They'd done a fantastic job of converting a ramshackle set of buildings into a brand spanking new brewery and visitor centre, all on time and within budget. We realised we ought to treat them for this unheard of accomplishment, and of course a night out in York seemed the best idea. It probably was, until some idiot suggested we take them to Toffs Night Club, just fifty yards or so along the road from us.

Smithy and I are only now, twenty years later, able to laugh about that night. For years we maintained an embarrassed silence. The memory was just too painful. We had no idea when we wandered in there – a bunch of lads with a median age of forty-five – that this was Grab-a-Granny night. But the Grannies certainly did, and they thought all their birthdays – their many, many birthdays, I should add, because there weren't many this side of seventy in the entire place – had come at once. By the time Smithy and I beat a retreat at two in the morning, we were smothered in lipstick and reeked of cheap perfume. As Smithy remarked, 'Bloody hell, the older they were the less they had on!' As to the builders, we left them to it. I had a suspicion they were quite enjoying the attention of a room full of geriatric sex maniacs.

Back in the world of brewing, we were now ready for 'gyle number one' as the first brew is known. Every vessel had been cleaned to within an inch of its life with caustic, then thoroughly rinsed with fresh water. The grist case was loaded up with twenty bags of malted barley and the water in the hot liquor tank was up to temperature, 90 degrees. The boiler was running as smoothly as it ever would, hissing and belching to Andrew's satisfaction. Our carefully selected strain of yeast had arrived to general rejoicing and been 'woken up' – that is, activated. I actually caught Andrew whispering to it, 'Get ready, your moment's about to arrive.' David Smith, who was going to stay with Andrew throughout the first brew, was present, and at seven o'clock on the morning of Friday 17th May 1996, production was under way. It was a memorable moment, not so much because of any ritual involved, more from the lack of it. Late that evening Andrew and David pitched the yeast into the coppered wort they'd collected in fermenter number 1. They then glanced at the clock – it was 10.30 – and agreed we just had time for a quick pint in the Falcon before they closed.

Waiting for that brew brought back long-forgotten memories of being an expectant father in a maternity hospital: desperate for things to turn out right, anxious for the mother – in this case our esteemed brewer – but unable to do much more than pace the building from end to end, my forehead wrinkled and my face contorted into an anxious grimace. Of course I couldn't resist asking Andrew how it was going every so often – like two or three times an hour – and he was constantly trying to find new ways of telling me to be patient, because there was nothing to report, which was good news. A few days later, after he'd transferred the beer from the fermenter to the conditioning tanks we'd see him running it off into a jug from time to time, smelling the contents, sometimes sipping them and gazing thoughtfully at the ceiling. Surely he could give me an update? Surely he had some indication how it was working out? But all I got was an enigmatic smile, or a cautious thumbs-up. Was he being cagey, or cautious? Was he winding me up? Was he already suffering brain damage as a result of some ghastly miscalculation in the alcohol content? The longer I waited for an outcome, the more it seemed that all four might be possible.

Slowly the days ticked by, and we waited for him to rack

the first brew into casks. Then I dashed around the place feverishly, finding things to do to take my mind off the fact that there, in that pile of second hand steel containers, was the fruit of a long year's endeavours, the first-born child we had waited and worked so hard to create. How long before we could select a cask, get the hammer, knock in the spile and tap it?

Finally, with my personal deadline upon us – June 1st 1996 – the historic moment arrived. The first brew of what was to be Yorkshire Terrier was ready to try. There was no fanfare, no roll on the drums, just Andrew crooking his finger and summoning me and Smithy to the bar area. He'd connected a cask up to a hand-pump, and had three pint glasses lined up. With a gesture of his hand he invited me to fill them.

Out it came, pale, lively, with a rich aroma of yeast and hops. I remember holding mine to the light, tapping it against Smithy's glass, and Andrew's. Then it was, 'Cheers, lads!' and down she went. As I swallowed the contents I was reminded of the place where this whole adventure began, the time Kevin and I visited the brewery at Lastingham. If that beer was a revelation, the opening of a door into an imagined future, this one was pure, joyous, satisfaction.

'That,' I said, 'is one hell of a pint. Fill her up again, landlord.'

When Smithy and I set out on this adventure we were thinking of making a quality beer. It soon occurred to us that we needed more than one brand. Quite how many was a question for a later date. We also realised that we'd need to name our beers. But first, variety. Each different type of beer you brew requires its own recipe of malted barley, and its own species of hops. So restricting ourselves to two beers made a lot of sense in the early days.

Smithy and I had a couple of brand names in mind, but

Kevin had told us about a contact he had, a fellow called Nick
Townsend. He worked for an outfit called BCA Consulting
Group, a marketing company based in York. 'They're good,'
he assured us, and then, just as we got interested he added,
'but they're not cheap.' I knew it made sense to get some
proper professional advice. Branding is not for amateurs. So
I trotted up to their offices and met this guy, Nick. It was a
useful discussion which bore fruit in the shape of a very fair
deal. He would submit quotations for designing a company
logo, letterheads, beer mats and compliments slips. He would
also come up with names for our first two brews. I did
mention our own suggestions, but he declined to comment. I
think he didn't want to sound rude. The deal was that if we
still preferred our own ideas there would be no charge; if we
wanted his they would cost £200 apiece. I walked away
thinking I'd done well. We'd surely stick to our names.

A few days later Smithy and I sat down to see Nick's
presentation on the artwork he'd come up with. We loved his
idea for a brand logo. In its original form it incorporated the
City of York's own motif – the red cross on a white
background with five gold lions. As a matter of courtesy I
called the City Council to advise them on what we were
doing. It never occurred to me that I needed to seek their
permission. How wrong can you be? A few days later I got a
call from some pen-pusher telling me in no uncertain terms
that I had no right to use the City's emblem. To be fair to the
guy, he was well within his rights – and he was, unwittingly,
doing us a favour. We put our heads together and replaced
the lions with five barrels, our soon-to-be iconic image.

As to names, we fell instantly in love with Nick's first
suggestion, which was 'Yorkshire Terrier'. It fitted perfectly
with the beer we were aiming for, which would be 'A
premium bitter with a rich, creamy malt and full hop palate

finish'. We wanted a bitter, hoppy brew with an ABV – that is, Alcohol By Volume – of 4.2 per cent. To ensure the dry, hoppy finish, which gave the beer a distinctive bite, we used exclusively Challenger hops. So 'Terrier' seemed spot-on. It suggested a slightly cheeky brew, something to put a smile on your face when you saw the name for the first time. Paying Nick for his time on that one was no problem.

The second name was a bit more problematic. Smithy and I had toyed with the idea of having one of the more playful names we'd started to see in the mid-90s, like 'Brewer's Droop', but after some thought we decided that quirky wasn't quite our style. We wanted people to choose our beers for their intrinsic qualities, not because they wanted to impress their mates as they ordered a pint of 'Dog's Bollocks'. Nick suggested 'Stonewall', his idea being that it would conjure up an image of the city's ancient limestone walls. Yes, we said, but it's also the name of the gay campaigning organisation. Not that we had a problem with that as such, but the beer-drinking public might not take to it. We considered going back to our original choices, 'York Bitter' or 'Ebor Ale', but realised that having either of them next to 'Yorkshire Terrier' would make it all seem a bit parochial, which was one reason why we settled for Stonewall. As for the beer itself, we used crystal malt, which gave it a darker colour and a richer, sweeter flavour. My tasting notes described it as 'A smooth, creamy session bitter with full malt character and hop undertones'.

Choosing hops is no simple task. There are so many varieties, each with its unique characteristics; and even when you've settled on a particular type, the taste can vary from one harvest – or even one field – to the next. To get Stonewall the way we wanted it, we went for a mixture of Fuggles and Challenger.

It's worth pointing out here that the process of coming up with a new beer isn't as complicated as it might seem. What you basically do is pick a beer that's already on the market that you like. First you try to emulate it, then improve it. The fact is that we based Terrier on Timothy Taylor's Landlord, but toned down its essential 'hoppiness' and made it a little sweeter on the palate.

Having got a couple of names we would be happy to sell, we needed the paraphernalia that went with them. It's hard to get excited about plastic pump-clips, but it's the little details that help build up the overall profile of a product. Landlords won't buy your beer unless you have the clips. They want their customers to see the options available, by name, as they walk up to the bar. Besides, it gives the more imaginative brewers a chance to show off their marketing prowess. So there's no avoiding them. In any case, they're knocked out by the manufacturers – in our case Colour Scan in Burton on Trent – for a few coppers apiece.

As time went by we would be casting around for more names for our beers. We realised we had to be careful. It's all too easy to come up with a name and discover when it's too late that it belongs to some other company. It happened to us some years later, after we'd started opening our own pubs around town. As soon as the Three-Legged Mare opened in High Petergate the locals christened it the Wonky Donkey. It didn't take us five minutes to decide we needed a product of the same name, so we bottled up a run of beer with a picture of a suitably dopey looking quadruped on the label and stacked it behind the bar. A few days later I got a call from the owner of Goose Eye, a Keighley brewery, a super guy named Jack Atkinson. I'd met him at a number of beer festivals and other events, so we knew each other well enough by this time. 'Did you realise I've already got a

Wonky Donkey?' he said. Without thinking I answered, 'You want to get yourself to the doctor, mate.' 'No,' he said, 'a beer. I have a beer called Wonky Donkey.' I apologised, of course, at which he said, 'But if you want to put up a cask of it – just in that pub – I won't have any complaints.' While all the small breweries are naturally in competition, there is a genuine camaraderie, and, by and large, we treat each other well.

The Yorkshire Wildlife Trust had their premises right next door to us in Toft Green, so we knew them well enough, and when it came to their fiftieth anniversary they asked us whether we'd do them a special brew and make a donation to the Trust: ten pence for each pint we sold. I said sure we would, so long as they came up with a name and did the artwork for the pump clip. They had a think and came up with Badger Bitter.

It didn't take me long to recall that there was a brewery by that name down in Dorset, actually a very old firm dating back to the 1770s who had a chain of around 250 pubs. I picked up the phone and gave them a call. I asked very politely whether we could use the name as a one-off in a good cause. They answered equally politely that we couldn't. The Trust soon came up with an alternative. Unfortunately it was Gannet. Why anybody would buy a pint of Gannet was beyond me, but it was their call and we went with it. But don't ever tell me that marketing is fun.

We knew that ultimately we planned to have several brews to our name, but right now, with these first two, we felt we were up and running. We didn't envisage brewing anything else for some time. We fully expected our reputation to spread like wildfire, and on the back of that to expand the business at a pace we could cope with. Deliveries would be within a thirty-mile radius. We thought it would all run very smoothly, a measured, controlled rate of progress. Looking back, I can see that if we really thought success was around the corner, we must have been round the bend. Selling beer just ain't that easy.

Joanne had sent out our first sales packs, consisting of pictures of the brewery, tasting notes on our beers, pump clips, and that enticing 'first order' offer that no landlord could refuse. It was at this point that the advice of Peter Frost started to make real sense. I recalled how he talked with feeling about the big brewers' – and the big pub chains' – closed-shop approach to independents.

Back in 1996 the only kind of pub whose landlord could decide for himself what beer to serve was that all but extinct species, the free house. There were in fact quite a few pubs that billed themselves as free houses – it was always a good selling point – but the fact is that most of them were no such thing. They were chain pubs, and the only freedom the tenant had was to choose from a list of beers put out by head office – brews from the big breweries, who could offer big discounts. The trouble was, the discounts were offered to the owners of the chain, not to the landlords direct. The landlords paid what head office told them to pay. End of story. Typically, in those days, head office would be creaming off £100 to £140 per 36-gallon barrel. Do the sums – or let me do them for you: it added up to a rake-off of close to 50 pence a pint before it got as far as the customer's glass.

At this time, companies like Punch Taverns and Enterprise owned thousands of pubs between them, a situation in part due to the government's Beer Orders of 1989. This unfortunate piece of legislation, inspired by the fact that six major brewers had almost the entire pub trade stitched up between them, was designed to ensure that any brewery that owned more than a certain number of pubs had to sell a guest beer. The brewers looked at the new law, went and had a chuckle, then sold off thousands of pubs to new companies who used their market clout to buy the same beer from the same breweries at vastly reduced discounts, keeping a chunk for themselves while charging the tenants the full price.

The result of this upheaval was that the punter now had choice. 'Good evening, sir, and what would you like? We have this tasteless bland beer at the left-hand pump, sir, or this new tasteless bland beer from the right-hand pump, identified by its gaily coloured clip. Take your pick. And that'll be… let's see, twenty pence more than the last time you called in. Thank you very much indeed, squire.' Ker-ching!

The Beer Orders were well intentioned, but as so often when governments try to solve problems by drafting new laws they didn't think them through and the legislation backfired. The fall-out in this case was that a whole host of people took up tenancies, sold their houses, gave up jobs and withdrew savings to live a dream, and were soon unable to make a living. To the odd few, who knew what they were doing and chose the right pub, it was indeed a good life.

The same sort of scam is being enacted today. In my own local a couple with the right skills are working tirelessly to make a success of it. They've decorated the outside, tidied up the car park, put out hanging baskets full of flowers – and remembered to water them! The approaches are well lit at night, all the signs professionally made. You want to go in – and when you get inside you find a clean, well furnished set of rooms with decent, home-cooked food and a choice of five hand-pulled beers. They've worked wonders in the five years they've had the place, but now their tenancy is up for review and they're caught in the same old trap: according to the pub company they're doing so well that they can afford a massive increase in rent.

I was only tempted once to look at a tenancy, and that was when the Deramore Arms in Heslington became available. This was the pub in which Smithy and I had sat writing all those lists. I was sentimentally attached to it. So I made enquiries and invited a representative from Punch, the company that owned it, to come down to the brewery and talk it over. I assumed that I was embarking on a negotiation, with some give and take. I began with, 'So Punch will write into my contract that York Brewery can sell its full range of beers in the pub?' 'Certainly,' the rep said, 'but we'll charge you £140 per barrel of any beer you sell.'

I thought for a moment, then said, 'Okay, so let me get this straight. We're opening negotiations at £140 a barrel. Is that right?' 'Ah, no. That price is written in tablets of stone.' I digested that, then said, 'Okay, let's talk about the rent, shall we?' 'Sure, go ahead.' 'Well, if we're going to pay you a fortune each year for the privilege of selling our own beer, we're going to need a substantial reduction in the rent we pay.' He shook his head. 'No. The thing is, if you have your pump-clips all along the bar our pub – Punch's pub – is going to look as though it's a York Brewery house.' He looked at me. Never even blinked. Then he said, 'So we'll increase the rent accordingly.'

I gave it one more try. I'd taken half a morning away from my desk for this. 'I don't suppose that's up for negotiation?' I asked. He pursed his lips and frowned. 'No, that too is....' I finished his sentence for him. 'Written in tablets of stone. Okay,' I said, 'so can you offer me one good reason why I should have any interest in taking over the pub?' Again, he didn't need to think. 'No,' was all he said.

'Well,' I said, standing up and holding out my hand, 'thanks for coming to see me. Er, don't fancy a beer, do you?' 'Love to,' my man said. 'I really like your brews.'

Sorry, We Are *Not* Calling It 'The Dog's Bollocks'

Contrary to all advice, I'm a great believer in mixing business and pleasure. It's amazing what you can find out, talking to people who, with business hats on are complete tossers, but who, once they step into the bar turn out to be perfectly decent guys. The man from Punch and I got on very well once the conversation had turned to cricket, and the weather and – well, anything except the price of a pint.

So my opinion of pub companies at the time of setting up York Brewery was that they employed unfair business practices, that they were responsible for higher prices for a pint and invested less in the pubs they owned than the breweries had done in the past, that they weren't willing to train their landlords adequately in what was, if done correctly, a very skilful occupation. The net result was a huge number of pub closures all over the country. It's tragic to see how many villages now have no pub, and the fall-out is the destruction of small communities and the slow death of one of the most appealing aspects of British culture.

I appreciate, of course, that many pubs had to go. There were, quite simply, too many. But the greed of the pub companies has closed many viable ones. Their only yard-stick is the bottom line, profits.

On the plus side, pub companies have become more friendly towards the idea of selling cask ales over the past few years. They've finally recognised that there is a demand out there and have started introducing guest beer lists. They have negotiated vast discounts with the brewers on the back of promises of huge volume sales, usually through one of the main beer wholesalers. This has proved reasonably successful, but more is required – and it is coming in the shape of new legislation which will enable tenants of any pub owned by one of these companies to buy one guest ale at his own discretion. It will be a massive step forward.

Further down the road, Smithy and I would start to think about owning our own pubs, but for now, we exulted in the joy of running our own business. It was hard graft, it was uncertain, it was precarious – but I thanked my lucky stars daily for the fact that I no longer had to kowtow to a lot of senior managers who were employed as puppets and soon turned into muppets. We had to milk that sense of liberation for all it was worth, because we weren't making any money and had no idea when – if ever – we might. Andrew, Smithy and I had all agreed that we would take out no more than £10,000 a year each. I took comfort in the fact that if there was a problem it was our very own problem, mine and Smithy's – and we trusted ourselves to sort it out.

Our first challenge was to shift our first twenty barrels and get brewing again as fast as was humanly possible. Otherwise we were 'dead in the wort'. And we were convinced it would all be fine. We had the 'hook': buy one get one free. That couldn't fail, could it? Who would turn down an offer of free beer?

We got off to a good start. No denying that. That first brew sold out in no time – although of course half of it went for nothing. We hit the phones. We hit them hard – myself, Smithy, Roy and Joanne. We ploughed through all the local directories and called every bar, pub, licensed premises in Yorkshire. We promised all sorts of inducements: bar mats, bar towels, T-shirts and pens – none of which we possessed, but all of which we would rush out and buy the minute we started getting orders.

Our efforts were, eventually, rewarded – and what a good feeling that was. The irony was that, having started out with the idea of projecting ourselves as York's only brewery, we couldn't seem to find any takers in the city. There were so few genuinely free houses. The only regular sale we had in those early days was at The Maltings, a splendid pub down by the river, under Lendal Bridge.

It's worth pausing here to give a mention to Sean – and his wife Maxine. I'd approached him at an early stage in our planning. His was the only genuine free house in York that actually sold cask ale. They were pioneers in those days, dedicated to promoting the joy of a flavoursome, hoppy ale as opposed to the bland fizzy pop that came in kegs. Their pub was an oasis in a desert of crap beer. No wonder CAMRA members and other true beer-lovers beat a path to their door and sang their praises. They rightly received national acclaim – and still do, even though you're hard put to find a pub in York nowadays that doesn't have a few hand-pulls to choose from. Sean and his missus were typically forthright when I told them I was planning to set up a brewery just up the road from them. He told me that, even if we produced a good beer, it would be a tough market to break into – and we would have to offer consistency of quality at a very keen price. 'You bring me a bloody good beer,' he said, 'at a competitive price, and I promise you I'll keep a pump for York Brewery. And if it's shite, forget it.'

Sean remained true to his word. He sampled our new brew, gave it the thumbs up, and placed his order. If he knew who was going to deliver it he might not have been so keen. Smithy had as much experience as a drayman as I had as a brewer. When he arrived with that first cask he heaved it out from the back of the Renault, got it to the head of the cellar steps and, as per Sean's instructions, let it go. Only one problem: he hadn't checked that Sean was ready to catch it. It flew down the steps, bounced twice and hurtled across the cellar floor, only missing Mine Host because he had the good sense to leap to one side as he saw his nemesis bearing down on him. But Sean forgave him.

Unable to make any further inroads into the city, we started looking further afield. And further, which is how we ended up with regular runs north to Edinburgh and south to Braintree, down in darkest Essex. As we found the odd customer in places like Scarborough or Sheffield Smithy would call in on neighbouring pubs, or ones along the route, and pitch them our special 'BOGOF' offer. It wasn't long before we'd developed an east coast route which covered everywhere from Hull to Whitby.

Slowly the delivery network spread, into Lincolnshire and Oxfordshire, over the Pennines to Manchester Liverpool, and North Wales. Our next target was to get enough orders to sell a weekly brew – that is, twenty barrels or eighty firkins. We were gaining valuable insight into the psyche of the pub landlord. The biggest hurdle by far in dealing with these people – almost exclusively men – is getting to speak to them. They're slippery customers – elusive, frequently absent and, when you do corner them, evasive. When you're trying to sell beer, over the phone, the first thing you need to grasp is that the landlord – and I use the term loosely, to cover managers, tenants, leaseholders and freeholders – is simply never in. And even if he is in, you have to understand that he's not.

Nine times out of ten whoever answers the phone will tell you the man himself is 'at the bank', or 'playing golf', 'on holiday' or 'having a lie-down'. Half the time they're right there beside whoever's answering the phone. I remember calling the Gillygate pub in York one morning and getting the cleaning lady. 'Is Jim there?' I asked. She held the phone away from her mouth – but not far enough – and said, 'Jim, it's Tony from York Brewery. D'you wanna speak to him?' I could hear Jim's answer, plain as day. 'Nah, tell him I'm not here.' I was about to say, 'Okay love, I heard him. Tell him to have a nice day,' but she beat me to it. 'He says to tell you he's not here,' she said, and hung up.

So half the time we were beating our heads against the wall. A whole bunch of the landlords we'd call weren't allowed to buy from us; or they had a cosy relationship with some other brewery that 'looked after them' with free beer, tickets for football games and suchlike. Some of them didn't want the trouble of getting cask beer in. Either they didn't like it – which to my mind made them worthless tossers – or they were flat out lazy and just couldn't be bothered to go down to the cellar for a few minutes every day and look after it. But this was still the Dark Ages for beer drinkers, 1996. We had a long, long way to go yet.

10.
CASKS? THEY'RE NOTHING BUT A FIRKIN NUISANCE!

Our efforts on the phones had brought us some success, but threw up their fair share of problems too. Our initial break-even figure of ten barrels a week had now increased to fifteen – that is, sixty firkins, or nine-gallon casks. That meant that we needed thirty pubs taking two 'nines' a week. At this early stage most of our pubs were taking Stonewall or Terrier as guest ales. When we asked them how the sales were doing we generally got a really positive responsive. 'They're going great.' 'My regulars love it.' 'We sold out Saturday night.' This was music to our ears. It was what we'd dreamed of, the hope that kept us going as we ripped all those nails out of the brewery timbers and sluiced the muck out of that mound of ancient, grimy casks - the idea that people would buy the beer we'd created and fall in love with it. 'Great,' I'd say, and get my pen out. 'So how many will you want next week?'

'Oh, we've already got our guest rotation worked out. Give us a ring in a couple of months.' It hurt; it really did.

What were you supposed to do to achieve the breakthrough? At the same time as we were looking up at this brick wall erected by the majors, we had another problem looming. Cash flow. Selling beer is one thing. Getting landlords to pay for it is a whole other ball-game.

And then there was the issue of casks. By the time we started brewing Steve, the lad that Wraggy had sent us, had, with my assistance, emptied all our 250-odd casks of sludge, spiles, keystones and other debris. They'd all gone through Andrew's rigorous cleaning process – twice, as per his orders. On the outside they looked what they were, second-hand casks that had seen a bit of life. Their insides, however, were pure and spotless. No bugs anywhere.

Of course, once your cask gets into a dingy pub cellar it sort of loses its identity. It is one of many, and draymen, being what they are – in a hurry, not too fussy – will frequently scoop up any strays on the principle that in some other cellar one of their fellow draymen is likely making off with theirs. So we colour-coded each one and gave it a reference number. At that time there were no more than 300 small, independent breweries in the country, so that was workable. We decided on a thick band of burgundy around the middle, and a stencilled number on the top of each cask. A tedious job that Smithy's clan did for 50 pence an hour.

Casks from small breweries mostly come in two sizes: the eighteen-gallon, known as a kilderkin, and the nine-gallon, or firkin. There are others. There's the four-and-a-half gallon, or pin; the 36-gallon, which is the barrel, and the hogshead, at a whopping 54 gallons. But 90 per cent of our sales were firkins. Casks are made from one of three materials. Stainless steel is the most popular, being resistant to all kinds of mistreatment. Aluminium has the advantage of being lighter, but of course isn't as durable. And then there's plastic, widely used today but as recently as the mid-1990s practically unheard of.

We soon found that it was firkins, or 'nines', that the landlords wanted. We had about 110 eighteens, and 140 of the nines. Time and again we'd find a landlord who wanted two firkins and, naturally enough, we'd put it to him that an eighteen-gallon cask would meet his needs just as well – and when would they like it delivered? And time and again we'd hear the familiar answer. 'Thursday at ten. But I don't want an eighteen, I want two nines.'

Were these landlord simply being cussed, or was there a rational explanation? Time to ask our resident expert. I found him, on his knees, arse in the air, at the bottom of an empty mash tun. Even our esteemed head brewer had to take his turn at cleaning. 'Andrew,' I said, 'why are all these landlords asking for two nines rather than one eighteen?' It was simple – to him. 'Because nines last longer in the cellar. You don't have to allow air into the cask until late on with the second nine – and if it's selling slowly that matters. Different if you're getting through it faster. In that case an eighteen will do nicely.'

I wasn't sure that I followed his argument all the way, but he was the expert and he had a cleaning job to complete. It was pretty obvious that I needed to get hold of some firkins – and soon. Or convince our customers that our beer would sell fast enough to warrant it being delivered in eighteens. Maybe we should offer an eighteen at a better price, and if they passed on the discount to the drinking public, surely it would go faster and we'd all benefit. That worked, and it got us out of a tight spot.

I'd realised by now that for me to breeze into a pub and try sell to the landlord face to face was a waste of time. For one thing, I would spend way too long waiting for them to show up for an appointment – if they showed up at all. As we went through our lists of potential pub customers it slowly dawned on me that, rather than tackling one pub at a time, I ought to be looking at volume sales via wholesalers. The most interesting, from our point of view, was Wetherspoons – and a few other smaller companies who had their own chain of pubs and liked to take guest ales. With these people, I was happy to go in and meet face to face. They would have a dedicated beer purchaser, and I could make a firm appointment with him or her. These were people who knew far more about the business than I did, people from whom I could learn a great deal. Better still, the end result – if it worked out – was high volume sales.

I knew I couldn't do all this alone. I needed help. It was time to speak to Wraggy again. 'I need a sales person,' I started. 'Got to be female. Yes, I know it's not p.c., but landlords love to flirt on the phone, and we're a new business. We'll do whatever it takes, within the law.'

Wraggy followed my line of logic. 'So what other qualities?' he asked. 'What else has she got to be good at?'

'I want someone who can talk the hind leg off a donkey. Got to be resilient – you know, when they slam the phone down on her. Can't have one of these people who bursts into tears. She has to be ready to dial the next number and make it sound like the sun's shining and it's her first call of the day. You know, typical Yorkshire.' I waited for Wraggy to laugh, then carried on. 'I need someone who can talk them into submission – keep rabbiting on until they agree to buy the beer just to shut her up.' 'I get the picture,' he said, 'and I've got just the woman you're looking for.'

Carol showed up next morning at ten o'clock, as requested. It didn't take us long to realise that, for the sake of everyone's sanity, she should have her own office. Not that we were over-endowed with rooms, just that our new recruit quickly brought to mind that old saying, 'Be careful what you wish for.' We'd asked for a talker and that's what we got. And not just any talker. This girl could project – round corners, down corridors, across streets. With some of her local calls she could probably have managed without the use of the phone. So, approximately five minutes after she arrived, I made an executive decision. Andrew's office would now be the sales office. He would have his very own dedicated filing cabinet in the corner, and use of the phone. Well, he wasn't crazy about admin; and he was far too busy brewing, cleaning out the vessels, skimming the yeast from the top of the fermenters and transferring the brew into the conditioning tanks. I wouldn't say he was allergic to Carol, but we soon noticed that if he had to use the office he chose to do so before she arrived or after she'd gone.

As well as trumpeting at people down the phone – I mean drumming up business – Carol was responsible for ensuring that our drayman had his next day's deliveries racked up, ready to be loaded into the faithful old Renault van, otherwise known as 'the rust-bucket'.

Carol was good at her job. She got results. But good news is never wholly good. As the orders mounted we were confronted with a serious cask shortage. Our weekly break-even target was growing all the time. At fifteen barrels we would be sending out sixty firkins a week. But when we factored in the amount of time each one was out – either in transit, in storage, in use, or sitting there empty awaiting pick-up – it was plain that we needed an awful lot more. Add the fact that drayman often picked up the wrong casks by accident or design; tot up all the empties that were now in various paddocks holding up red-and-white poles so that somebody's daughter could leap across them on her show-pony, and I soon came to the conclusion that for every cask we had in the brewery at any one time there might be another eight scattered around our ever-extending patch. But by the time I'd done that calculation I'd have Roy telling me he'd been on the computer and had a revised break-even figure, so maybe I ought to adjust my figures accordingly. Upwards.

A friend from our Little Chef days, Alan Robinson, had a friend who worked for Boddington's in Manchester. This guy, on hearing of our cask crisis, was determined to help. One of his duties was to dispose of casks that were deemed too old or knackered for their use – whereas we, of course, couldn't give a toss what they looked like. Our only concern was, how many, and how much? Alan's mate reckoned he had about a hundred – certainly too few for an outfit like Boddington's to miss. As for a price, it was a matter of 'Come and fetch them – and stand me a few pints.'

We couldn't believe our luck. Within a couple of days we'd collected 112 casks and were busy washing them out, painting them in new colours and stencilling YORK BREWERY on them. It was only when Smithy had driven all the way to Scarborough and was about to make his first drop-off that we found out the awful truth. He opened the rear doors to find the casks barely visible through a mist. Numerous pin-prick holes were letting out a fine spray of beer, which was already an inch deep on the van floor.

Back at the brewery we tried any number of commercial sealants, but none worked. We had no choice but to do what Alan's mate was supposed to do in the first place: scrap them. It was all the proof we needed of that saying, 'If something looks too good to be true, it probably is.'

So the cask problem remained unsolved. We were still no nearer to finding a supplier or the means to pay them. Somehow we managed to track down a French company

called Villeneuve who could produce nine-gallon firkins with our name painted on, and each one bearing its number on a metal plate which was permanently welded to the cask. That was the good part. The bad part was the price: £50 a throw – and, even worse, they were the cheapest I could find. But… needs must. We took a deep breath, and placed an order for a hundred. I remember me and Smithy waiting for them on the day they were supposed to arrive. They were needed for an order we'd promised for the very next day. Six o'clock came and we had to let Steve go. He'd been hard at it all day. Andrew was knackered and left soon after. His parting shot was, 'Don't forget to put those new casks through the wash procedure. Twice.' We glared at him. 'Brand new,' he said. 'They'll need it.' Cheers, Andrew. And sleep well. Slave-driver.

We spent the evening pacing up and down and calling the couriers. Don't worry, we were told. They're on their way. They were, and they showed up at midnight. By the time we'd washed them – twice, as per our brewer's orders – and racked them with beer, the sun was rising. It pained us to part with £5,000 – and we knew that worse was around the corner. If we did as we needed to, and upped production level to the twenty-barrel mark, we'd need yet more of them. 640 to be precise. I dried my eyes, blew my nose and went into battle once more.

Buying the remainder of what we required at this price was a non-starter. We simply didn't have the cash. '£32,000?' Smithy said. 'You're having a laugh.' What we really needed was what they like to call 'blue sky thinking'. It's not a phrase I particularly liked. I'd heard enough bullshit from senior management at Little Chef, and that sort of talk was all part of it – fancy language designed to impress you that they had some clue as to what they were talking about.

What happened next was in any case more like 'pennies from heaven'. From somewhere at the back of my mind came a recollection of a conversation I'd had with David Smith. He'd mentioned The Old Mill Brewery, a Goole firm which, he reckoned, were experimenting with plastic casks. Actually, they were between Goole and Pontefract, in a tiny little place called Snaith. The casks weren't supposed to be used in the general trade, but The Old Mill was well established, having been founded in 1983, and had their own estate of about ten pubs. I got on the phone and asked to speak to the boss. I actually got his son on this occasion, a lad called Mark Wetherall who would later succeed his dad.

'Hi,' he said, 'how can I help you?' I took a deep breath, explained my problem. 'I understand you use plastic casks. Is that right?' Mark told me that his dad not only owned the brewery but also a plastics factory, and that he'd been developing a lightweight plastic cask for years. The original intention, he said, was to develop a disposable container.

However, this latest model was more robust and could be re-used. He'd now got to the point where he was trialling them in their pubs. This sounded like the kind of thing we needed - in huge quantities. I asked him whether he would consider dropping a couple off at our place and letting us test them. To my surprise, he agreed. They arrived the very next day.

We started by putting them through the cleansing process. The first thing we noticed was how much easier this was than with the metal ones. They were far better to handle. There were a couple of other minor drawbacks – like the shives bouncing halfway down the yard when you whacked them, but the lightness and, of course, the price, overrode any reservations we might have had. Our big worry was that the plastic might taint the beer, so we filled them both to see what the result was after a few days. Some serious sampling – that is, slowly quaffing our beer at the end of a day's work and savouring its taste – revealed that it was fine. And, it seemed, so long as we handled the casks with care and didn't go hurling them down into the cellars, they could be used time after time.

So much for the positives. There were two vital questions still unresolved – and the answers would have a major bearing on the ever-present cash-flow crisis. The first was, could Old Mill manufacture all the casks we wanted? Because we wanted a lot, and we wanted them fast. On that we awaited an answer.

The second question was, how would the trade take to seeing their beer arrive in black plastic containers? That too would be a matter of waiting and seeing. Meanwhile, we turned our attention to the ever pressing cash-flow.

11.
BOTTLING IT

I had already been on my hands and knees to our lovely bank manager Stuart and convinced him to increase our overdraft limit from £10,000 to £20,000. Now I was asking him to raise it to £30,000. He reminded me sternly of what he'd told me at the outset: not to grow too fast. There was a limit to what the bank could do, and we had reached it. At £30,000 we were sailing close to the wind – as was he. Maybe I was more persuasive than I realised: I'd just got Customs and Excise to delay for two weeks our last monthly payment of beer duty, although I couldn't see them agreeing to it again.

Stuart pondered my situation and came up with a suggestion that would save our bacon. I'd never heard of factoring before, and he had to explain what it was. 'It's a procedure whereby a finance company, upon receiving a copy of the invoices you've sent out to your clients, immediately pays 80 per cent of the total due into your bank account.'

I sat there, mouth open and stared at him. 'My God!' I said. This sounded like the U.S. cavalry riding to the rescue. Our rescue. 'And as soon as your customer pays up,' Stuart continued, 'you get the remaining 20 per cent that's owing.' I was still struggling for words. 'And the catch?' I said. 'There has to be a catch. Surely.' Stuart sat back in his chair. 'Well, there'll be a set-up charge of about £2,500 per annum – plus a service charge. Say 2 per cent of your total invoices.' He paused. 'But you'll need to negotiate that with them.' 'Them?' I said. 'Who's them?' 'Ah,' he said, 'actually we have our own factoring arm within Nat West Bank.'

While all this was going on, Carol was doing a fantastic job of selling our beer. Such a good job in fact that she was costing us a fortune in diesel. With York's lack of free houses, and with the pub groups unwilling to take our brews locally she was having to look further afield – and then further still. In those early days, thanks to a relationship we'd built up with a couple of wholesalers down south who had taken a fancy to our beer, we were making a lot of sales in Essex. At the same time I'd started a dialogue with a nationwide outfit called Beer Seller. They'd been making encouraging noises and I was keeping my fingers crossed that I could turn their interest into actual orders.

Andrew, meanwhile, was doing a great job of brewing, such a good job that Steve was running out of casks to wash and rack. But cash flow was sorted for a few weeks ahead – although it would become a problem again before long - so on the face of it we were doing well, well enough to be hiring more staff. It was clear that a man of Smithy's talents was wasted as a delivery-man. I needed to get him in the brewery, where he could help out with the admin. Being a drayman was great for his physique – I'd never seen him look so svelte – but he hadn't mortgaged himself to the hilt in order to develop his six-pack. As ever, I called on my pal Wraggy. 'Now then,' I said, 'I need a drayman.'

'Okay,' he said, 'but you're going to have to tell me what a drayman is. What are his duties? I mean, give me an idea of a typical day in the life of.' 'Better take a seat,' I said. 'This could take a few minutes.' To tell the truth I had to give it some thought myself. I lit up a cigarette, then started. 'Okay, a drayman. Simple definition is... a bloke who delivers beer to our customers in our rusty old van. As to his working day....' I took a deep breath and continued. 'Well, he comes in at seven o'clock – earlier if he has a long way to go. He starts by loading said rust-bucket with casks full of beer – so he needs to be well made; good at lifting. And he needs an organised mind, so that he can load the casks in reverse order. First in, last out sort of idea. You got that?' Wraggy agreed that he had.

'Okay, next thing he needs to be is a good map-reader. Half the pubs are tucked away in villages way out in the sticks. The other half are up some ancient back-street in town – usually one-way. Then once he's found the pub he has to come over all smooth-talking – your perfect customer relations guy – because the odds are that whatever time of day you show up with your beer, the landlord is pissed off. Most of them start the day with a hangover, and hurling abuse at draymen perks them up.

'Anyway, once the landlord is up and dressed, the drayman can begin doing the thing he's come all this way to do – namely drop the beer into the cellar. Dropping is not a term to be taken literally. We're not talking open the hatch and kick the buggers through. It's a bit more scientific than that.' I paused here to check that Wraggy was still listening. He assured me he was. 'Okay,' I said, 'casks have to be roped and lowered with great care. You don't want them to be damaged. Once they're in the cellar the drayman has to roll them along to the precise spot where the landlord wants them. All the while his eyes will be darting left and right, looking for stray casks – because once he's got his full ones in place he's going to have to rummage through the sixty-odd empties that will be scattered about the darkest corners of the cellar and fish out the ones belonging to York Brewery. With luck he'll find the same two that he brought several weeks ago. As often as not he will only unearth one, in which case he will cast aside his carefully cultivated customer relations persona and give it a bit of, 'Oi, landlord, where the fuck's that other cask? Don't you know we're running out of them and about to go bust, and I'll be out of a job? And by the way, the boss says you haven't paid for the last lot yet so we're having cash for this delivery, you `orrid little shit!'

'Hang about,' Wraggy said. 'Are you saying..?'

'No, scrub the last bit. It's just wishful thinking. Anyway, the process continues until your drayman has been to all the pubs on his list – plus a few more in the vicinity where he knows he can pick up the odd empty. But all that I've said so far is the tip of the iceberg. This man we're looking for is also going to need to pick up the many and varied skills of the cellar-man, because half the landlords he deals with won't know a damned thing about looking after our precious beer, so he's going to have to drum it into them that there's no future in them making a pig's ear of it and then sending us an ullage note when it's their own bloody fault.'

I lit another cigarette. 'Wraggy? Still there?' 'Yes,' he said. 'Just fetching some more notepaper.' 'Okay,' I continued, 'so now he drives back to the brewery, hungry, brain-dead and lathered in sweat. First job, he has to get all the empty casks out of the rust-bucket and manhandle them to the cask store. He will then clean up the vehicle. He'll tidy up the maps off the dashboard, and his newspaper, and his empty coffee cups and dirty gloves; then he'll tidy up all the spare spiles, beer mats, keystones and pump-clips he has to have ready for landlords who lose every bloody thing you ever send them. And just when he thinks it's time for home he'll grab all the invoices, along with any cash he's managed to extract from the grasping landlords' hands, and take it all to the office, where Roy or Smithy will ask him where the fuck he's been. He'll reply with a volley of abuse, tell them about any cash he's taken as payment, and let them know about any landlord who's not paid when he should've done.'

There was a long silence, then Wraggy said, 'That all?' 'No – he's got to have a clean driving licence.' I waited a few moments, took a deep breath and said, 'So what are the chances?' 'I have just the man you want,' he said. 'Only thing is, he's blind in one eye.' Wraggy didn't often crack jokes, and I thought he was serious. 'But it's not a problem,' he said. 'He has double vision in the other.'

Next morning a stranger walked into the brewery. Richard was about thirty years old, six-foot something tall, skinny as a rail and wore a beard - plus a suit that was two sizes too small for him. He had been a licensee with Yates' Wine Lodges. His grandfather had run the last coaching inn in the Nottingham area, at Carlton on the Hill. So he knew about beer. He was also a very keen photographer. He'd actually applied for a marketing job, but right now we needed to get him on deliveries. He was to be with us for nineteen years. He went out on the rounds with Smithy and soon gained an insight into the ways of landlords – and the Tony Smith technique for dealing with them.

Somehow we'd managed to get a clutch of customers down in Cambridgeshire, one of whom was a really unpleasant, foul-mouthed fellow. They called on him one morning and Richard went in to see if he was ready for them. Smithy was still in the van, catching up on the paperwork when he heard a commotion from inside the pub. 'What bloody time do you call this?' and so on. He was one of those: whenever you came it was wrong. Either they were in bed or busy doing lunches. The abuse continued until Smithy had heard enough. He stayed perfectly calm but shot from the hip. 'Excuse me,' he said, 'do you mind not talking to my driver that way? It's offensive, if you didn't realise it.'

A substantial row followed. I never got the details, just the outcome, but it seemed that the landlord blew his top. He huffed and puffed, and effed and blinded for several minutes. When he'd run out of steam he said, 'Right, I'm ready to take the beer now,' whereupon Smithy shook his head and said, 'No.' 'You what?' asked the landlord. 'I don't want to sell my beer to you,' Smithy said. 'You aren't worthy.' And with that he and Richard got in the van and left.

It wasn't always landlords who made life difficult for the drayman. Sometimes it was their customers. One Christmas we got a rush order from a pub in Acomb, just outside York. We were happy to oblige, even though the van was out. I sent Richard and Andrew out in my beat-up Lada. The pub was pretty beat-up too. As Andrew described it later, it was, 'The sort of place where stolen goods change hands on a regular basis'. As they hauled the beer inside, one of the regulars looked at the casks and pulled a face. He was an ugly bugger: grubby T-shirt, tattoos, pins in his face. He looked at Richard and said, 'Aye, and that's shite, that beer.' Richard looked at him, pointed at Andrew and said, 'Blame him. He brewed it.' Richard's recollection of those early days is of putting in twelve to fourteen-hour shifts. Smithy, who was always taking time out for a smoke, told him he ought to have a break too. Stumped for something to do, Richard started taking photos on the job – a practice that helped him develop the skills he now employs as a professional photographer in Tynemouth.

Not all landlords were awkward, far from it, but even when they tried to be helpful it didn't necessarily work out. Smithy had just completed a delivery to an Edinburgh pub, and was enjoying a laugh and a joke with mine host. As he was preparing to leave he asked him for directions to the next place he had to visit. 'Och mon, it's easy enough ye ken,' said the landlord, and then launched into a lengthy description of the route in broad Lowland Scots. Smithy, not having understood one word, replied as only Smithy would. 'Aye, now can you tell us again in fucking English?'

After Richard had spent a week or two on the road I asked Smithy how he was doing. 'Well,' he said, 'he's as mad as a box of frogs but you know what? I think he's going to enjoy it. Certainly enjoys driving.' 'What about all the abuse?' I said. 'From landlords.' 'Water off a duck's back.'

The following Monday Richard went out on his own and I was able to call Wraggy and congratulate him on another winner. 'Where do you find them?' I asked him. 'First Steve, the cask-washer and beer-racker, then Roy the book-keeper and office organiser; Carol the Sales Queen and now this drayman extraordinaire.' Wraggy didn't answer, but I did think I heard him purring down the phone.

We recruited quite a few draymen over the years, many of them fascinating characters. Bill Emberton had run several pubs around York with his wife Sue. At the time I met him they were in charge of the Punch Bowl in Stonegate. When they ran Ye Olde Starre Inn it became the first pub in the city to announce an annual turnover of a million pounds. Bill was a Scot, who'd come to York way back in 1962. He never lost his accent, nor his ridiculous sense of humour. His favourite joke was a riddle. 'Name a fish that begins with a 'k' and ends with a 'k'.' Of course, nobody ever had an answer. 'Kilmarnock,' he'd tell them. And of course he got the same response every time. 'That's not a fish.' To which Bill replied, 'It's a pla(i)ce, isn't it?'

Bill had plenty of high-profile visitors to the Starre. He loved to tell people about the time Luciano Pavarotti came in with a pair of stunning blondes and ordered three halves of lager; and of the actor Denis (*Minder*) Waterman who consented to having his photo taken with Bill, so long as Bill stood him a double vodka and tonic.

As you walk down Stonegate you can't miss the huge beam that spans the street, joining the Starre with the building opposite, and supporting both facades. The owner of the other place receives a token annual rent, which, by ancient agreement, he has to spend in the Starre, in the company of the landlord.

It was actually some years later, when we were working to create our own pub in Stonegate, that I got to know Bill. He told me that he was weary of running pubs and asked me, if anything turned up at the brewery, to let him know. When I mentioned that we could do with another drayman I never expected him to show the remotest interest, but within days he was down at Toft Green, studying a pile of maps in preparation for the day when he would quit his life-long career and come to work for us. With his background, he turned out to be the ideal man for the job, regularly passing on advice, and the benefits of his experience, to publicans he got to know on his rounds. Bill enjoyed his job so much that he worked on until he was seventy, retiring in January 2016.

Not all of our draymen got off to such as good start as Bill. I knew Simon Crawford as a fellow regular in the

Charles XII. He had been a driver with BRS truck rental, and had risen to the exalted position of National Operations Manager. He had taken early retirement, but was getting bored. He loved Yorkshire Terrier, which was now a fixture at the Charles, and wondered whether I might have an opening. We took him on part-time, but he was soon putting in a full week for us. He was to have mixed fortunes. He hadn't been on the job very long when he went to make a delivery at the Crown Inn at Dishforth. It was a freezing winter's day and the pub had a long, sloping, cobbled driveway. Simon parked at the top, pulled hard on the hand-brake and left the engine in gear. Then he went round to the back of the van, climbed inside and started re-arranging the casks. The movement prompted the van to start sliding down the driveway. All Simon could do was brace himself and hope for the best. He skidded the full length of the driveway, 150 yards but, despite his worst fears, came to rest without doing himself – or the van – any physical harm.

Simon wasn't so lucky a year or so later when he was on his way back from Birmingham with a load of empty casks. He was on the M1, approaching the turn-off for Chesterfield, when he saw a line of red lights up ahead – and there, right up against the central reservation on the southbound carriageway, a stationary car, with its driver's door open. Beside it, next to the crash barriers, was a man on foot. Simon slowed down as he approached the scene, but was still travelling at a fair speed when the man climbed onto the barrier and launched himself at the van. On impact, he bounced off the bonnet, and onto the windscreen, bending it to within six inches of Simon's face before slipping under the still moving vehicle.

The guy died instantly. It later transpired that he had a history of emotional difficulties. The police were very good with Simon, taking the trouble to assure him he had done nothing wrong, and praising him for his quick action in slowing down, and thereby avoiding a multiple pile-up. An air ambulance soon landed on the motorway to take the deceased man away, and the police insisted that Simon be taken to Sheffield Hospital to be checked over.

Three hours later he took a cab back to York. On the way, the driver told him that there had been a major hold-up earlier, the result, as he put it, of 'some twat killing a pedestrian'. Simon calmly advised his driver that he was 'that twat', then told the whole story to a very contrite cabby. Simon was back at work two days later, but didn't feel ready to go out on the road immediately. For a week or so he went on the rounds with Bill. The idea was to ease him gently back into the routine – but, he reported, it was the second most frightening experience of his life as a driver. I never did work out whether he was joking.

We'd eased the staffing situation – and, of course, added to our outgoings – but the most pressing concern was still the shortage of casks. I got onto Mark at the Old Mill Brewery. I told him that we'd trialled the two plastic ones he'd sent and asked what sort of price he had in mind were we to order, say, 200 – and when he could deliver. He reckoned he could get them to me in two weeks at £11.50 a throw. Quite an improvement on £50 for the steel ones.

A few days later we got the call we'd been hoping for. Beer Seller wanted a consignment of Yorkshire Terrier for delivery to ten of their depots about four weeks later. The size of the order took me aback. They wanted fifty nines to each depot, of which they had ten, making a total of 500 firkins. That was a genuine wow! moment.

Naturally, I couldn't wait to share the good news with our head brewer – and maybe tell him about another bright idea I'd had. He wasn't exactly bowled over. 'Six brews just for them?' He shook his head. 'Over six brews if you do the sums. I'm going to struggle – unless I get some help.'

Something about that weary shake of his head told me the other idea could wait. I had a good head brewer, and I needed to keep him sweet. No, I need to correct that. Some years later, when Andrew left York to go into the hop business down in Worcestershire, the word in the trade was that York Brewery had let go 'probably the most talented brewer in the U.K.'

The idea that was growing in my head was that we should start to bottle the Yorkshire Terrier. To me it made perfect sense. With no casks involved it would be a breeze, wouldn't it? There was, as ever, a fly in the ointment. We didn't have our own bottling plant and would have to deal with an outside firm, Robinson's. They would come with a tanker and take it off to their own place. Their minimum run would be for fifty barrels, or two-and-a-half of our brews – meaning yet more work for Andrew. Which was why I decided not to break the good news to him just yet. Besides, I had other things on my mind.

I called Mark and told him I was going to give him a firm order for plastic casks, but I needed them within two weeks. Could he do that? 'I think so,' he said. 'How many?' 'Five hundred,' I said. 'At £11 apiece.' 'Bloody hell. I'll talk to production and get back to you. But the price is fine.'

If he delivered, we were going to be in business. We had the big order from Beer Seller, and with the factoring business up and running we would get a whopping great cheque as soon as we delivered. And we'd saved twenty grand on casks. There was just one teeny little problem: we had yet to break it to Beer Seller that they'd be getting the beer in plastic containers. Andrew, not the wildest of optimists, was convinced they'd send it straight back. I preferred to think they'd query it, and I was confident I could persuade them. After all, Old Mill had been using them for over a year, and we'd been a hundred per cent satisfied with our own test. Andrew remained dubious. But, as he said, at least we're shifting beer.

No sooner had we started sending it out in the plastic casks than the phone started ringing. The first call was from our friends at Beer Seller. 'These casks you've sent,' they began. 'Yes?' I said. 'They're plastic.' I had prepared my spiel. 'Yes!' I said. 'Fantastic, aren't they? Brand new ones too. Straight from the factory. And the way we saw it, what with you being the leading beer wholesaler in the country – well, naturally we wanted you to have first crack at them. We wanted you to have the honour of the first batch.' 'But why didn't you warn us?' 'Ah. That was the surprise factor. It's really the only way to trial a new concept. We wanted honest off-the-cuff feedback from all your clients. And we decided this was the way to get it. No hard sell, just see what your people think. I mean, you're selling on to loads of different pubs, all over the country. They'll soon let us know what they think. Don't get me wrong, we've been trialling them and we're sold on them. They're great. No problems at all. So if you get a single customer complaining, just let me know and I'll deal with them direct.'

They agreed to accept the casks on condition that I would indeed handle any negative feedback – and that they reserved the right to refuse them in future if they didn't prove satisfactory. I did get a few complaints, mostly from landlords who found them too light. That had me baffled, until they explained that when they tapped the beer the cask would shoot off the stillage. I advised them to knock the tap through the keystone while the cask was still upright, and then lay it on the stillage. There were also one or two returns – generally ones that had been left standing in full sun. These had expanded to such an extent that the casks were almost perfectly spherical. De-pressuring them was a matter of 'Give it a light tap and stand well back.'

So we got away with it, and the casks were accepted by the majority of our customers. Their life was limited, of course, although in most cases we got ten or more re-fills. They were never going to replace stainless steel, but they got us out of a big hole and I'll forever be grateful to Mark at the Old Mill. We ended up buying 3,000 off him – and storing them in the roof space above the offices. In fact, as far as I'm aware some of them are still there, so if anybody has a use for them I'm sure the present brewery owners would welcome a call.

Our next job, of course, was to put a smile on our head brewer's face. He was casting gloom around the place, and it would only be lifted if we could find him an assistant – pronto. As it happened, the solution was staring us in the face. Nick Webster was a carpet fitter from Knaresborough. A keen home brewer, he'd been coming in on his days off and helping out, just for the experience. We'd only known him a few weeks but he'd made it plain that he was desperate to get into brewing full-time. Andrew, when we talked to him, said he would be more than happy to take him on full-time.

The new appointment made sense in more ways than one. Not only was Andrew under increasing pressure as our order-book filled up, but what if he got ill – or decided he'd had enough? Or wanted a holiday? The extent to which we relied on him was very much on my mind after a nasty incident one morning. I was trying to persuade Lanchester Wines of Tow Law, County Durham, to buy our beer. I heard an almighty crash from down in the brew-house. I couldn't just hang up, but when I noticed clouds of white powder rolling in through my half-open door I made my excuses and ended the call.

I rushed out onto the balcony and met Andrew, staggering up the stairs all covered in white. 'The grist case!' he gasped. 'Bloody thing's just collapsed.' He was lucky. He'd been standing right under it when his phone rang. As he went to answer, down came the case, along with twenty 25-kilo bags of malted barley – total weight half a tonne. When Andrew shook his head and said, 'I could've been killed,' I looked at the mess on the floor where he'd been standing a minute earlier and had to agree. After the dust had settled, I was left to reflect that this could indeed have been a fatal blow. Further investigation revealed that the bolts that held the grist case in place simply weren't robust enough. I immediately got the builders back to install a set of steel posts. Nothing short of a charge of Semtex, they assured us, would shift it now.

After the accident it didn't take me and Smithy long to decide we would hire Nick full-time. He was delighted to receive an offer and said he could start as soon as he'd worked his notice. With him in place I could now broach that tricky subject I'd been wanting to bring up. I sat Andrew down and opened the batting. 'Look,' I said, 'selling cask beer is a pain in the rear end. And it's risky. We've got all our eggs in one basket. What I want to do is diversify, open up new markets.' Andrew rolled his eyes. 'Yeah, I get it,' he said. 'You're talking about bottling, correct?' 'Exactly.'

Andrew then set about trying to unnerve me with a lot of stats about the costs involved. And to be fair he had some terrifying figures at his disposal. 'First off, you need someone to design your labels,' he said. 'That's cost number one. Then there's buying the labels themselves. We're talking a minimum of 30,000 a time. As for bottles – well, outrageous prices. Plus the caps.' He shook his head and put on his doleful face, but agreed to talk to Robinson's and get some prices. Meanwhile I would get to work on the labels.

I found a company called Darley's, well known throughout the brewing sector for producing decent labels at reasonable cost. I called a few local designers and asked them to send me their ideas. They were all keen to help, even when I explained that I wanted rough sketches at this stage and would only pay for the design I chose to go with.

We soon decided that Robinson's prices were good for us. I picked a design and we were ready to go – once we'd got our fifty barrels brewed. They would occupy all but one of our four fermenters, so there was no time to lose.

Although they weren't producing the labels for us, Robinson's were able to advise us on some of the legal issues involved. We were required to state the ingredients, the ABV, and the best before date. They also discussed bottle caps. Had we decided on a particular colour? No, it had never occurred to me. Neither had the idea of putting some text on them, but when they suggested it I came up with the title of a Rolling Stones song I used to listen to in the 1960s, 'Walking the Dog'. I thought it was a neat joke – as in, 'I'm just going to pop out with the dog, dear' – but of all the customers I saw uncapping a bottle of Terrier over the years I only ever met one who actually 'got it' and acknowledged what I always thought was a cute and subtle bit of marketing.

As the days ticked by we now needed to figure out what we were going to do with around 16,000 bottles of beer. While I chewed on that, Andrew and Nick rigged up the requisite hoses and pumps required to transfer the brew into Robinson's tanker when it showed up. Once loaded, it would be shipped to their bottling plant at Bradbury, near Stockport, where it would be pumped into coolers, tested in their lab, then bottled and capped. They would return to us sixteen pallets, each containing eighty-five cases (twelve 500 ml bottles per case). All we had to do was find somewhere to store it, then sell it. But at least it wouldn't go off – not for at least a year. In that respect we had time on our side.

Things were on the up, but our cash problem persisted. Fawcetts of Castleford, our malt suppliers, were still insisting on cheques being cleared before they would deliver – and wouldn't relent until we'd proven our reliability over a twelve-month period. Our accountants had just drawn up a profit-and-loss account for our first nine months' trading and shown that, despite sales worth £150,000, we'd made a loss of £35,000. Robinson's would want paying, and we would shortly be sitting on this mountain of bottled beer with no customers in sight.

The day of the shipment, Andrew checked his hoses and supervised the pumping. After the tanker drew away he emptied the hoses and collected two gallons of beer, which mysteriously disappeared that same afternoon, as did he.

Our York pubs: The Three Legged Mare, *above,* and The Rook and Gaskill, *right,* helped make our name

Left: The Last Drop Inn, our first pub

Street scene: The Terrier's superb tiled façade puts most of its Stonegate neighbours in the shade

Building for the future: York Brewery, before and after. God knows how we got that vat in, but we did!

Calendar girls: Cass Donato and Seona McLinden getting to the bottom of the brewing business for our charity calendar

© *The Press, York*
www.yorkpress.co.uk

Gold medalists: Winners at the Great British Beer Festival, *left to right*, Nick Webster, John Buckle, yours truly, Andrew Whalley and Bill Emberton

Our first team, early days: Joanne, myself, Richard, Steve, Andrew and Smithy

Full steam ahead: Gibbo gets to grips with the cask cleaning

Roll out the barrel: Our first York customer, and one of our most loyal, Sean Collinge at the Maltings

Above: Me with those legendary plastic casks.
Pictured right: Andrew Whalley, creator of champion beer Centurion's Ghost Ale, receives his commemorative 'pin' from Michael Parsons, editor of *The Brewer International*

© The Press, York
www.yorkpress.co.uk

Strength to strength: the opening of the Three Legged Mare, *left*; Yours truly chalking up another customer, *above*

Hard at work:
Nick and Gary
loading the
grist case, *above.*
Main image:
Andrew,
introducing
hops into the
copper, Nick
and Gary at the
mash tun

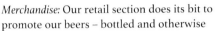

Merchandise: Our retail section does its bit to promote our beers – bottled and otherwise

Called to the bar: In-house hospitality. The bar extension *above left*, original bar, *left*, our man in Singapore, *above*

Changing times: Julie and me behind the bar, *left*, while Smithy and I welcome the new owners – by which point I reckon we deserved that pint...

Suited and booted: Smithy and I are presented with the Small Business of the Year Award – an achievement of which everyone at York Brewery was proud

12.
AN ANGEL DESCENDS
FROM THE HEAVENS

It was at this point that an angel entered my life. Not my missus, whom we'll come to later, but another woman, who arrived out of the blue and gave us the biggest boost we'd had so far. It would only be good manners to name our saviour, but the fact is that although I can still see her and hear her voice I haven't a clue what she was called. I remember two salient facts about her. One is that she was once captain of York Ladies Rugby Union team; the other is that she was manager of the wholesale catering unit at Nurdin and Peacock – and that's why I'd contacted her, to see whether we might do business together.

Nurdin and Peacock was a very large-scale outfit with an illustrious history. It was founded in 1810 by a French immigrant who'd made his fortune importing eggs from his native country and selling them in England. Later the firm was a pioneer in Britain's cash-and-carry business and soon became the leader in the field, until Booker took it over some years ago. I was feeling pretty nervous as I breezed into their store at Clifton to meet this woman. However, things went quite well and when I suggested she call in at the brewery and have a look at what we did, she agreed. She seemed to fall in love with the place. More importantly, when she tried the beer she gave it the thumbs-up. 'So,' I asked, 'would you like to order some?' She would.

Now, a pallet of beer contains over a thousand bottles, so when I put on my cheeky grin and asked her how many pallets she wanted, I was flying a kite. 'How many do you have?' she asked. 'Fifteen,' I said. 'And where are they?' 'At Robinson's in Stockport.' And then, in full cheeky monkey mode, I added, 'We can ship them direct to you if you'd prefer.' She never batted an eyelid. 'Smashing,' she said. 'You can expect the order from me this afternoon and I'll take delivery next week. Of the lot.'

A few days later the order was executed, our invoice to the factors was dealt with, and two days after that a whopping great cheque was deposited in our bank account. We were able to pay Robinson's, Darley's, the maltsters and, of course, our dear friends at Customs and Excise. Suddenly, being in business was fun again – and our reputation as prompt payers gained added lustre.

We'd actually let our angel take all but one of the pallets received from the bottlers. The remaining one allowed Carol to sell the odd case to restaurants, off-licences and hotels, and send out samples to supermarkets – or rather to their beer purchasers at head office.

While we slowly found our feet on the brewing and marketing side, I was still chewing over my original idea of having a show brewery. By July we were up and running. Staffed by Wraggy's Wonders, we were brewing,

grafting away and getting orders. Okay, we were making a loss, but we would soon sort that out. The only way was up, wasn't it? It was time, I announced, to tackle this visitor business before the we hit peak season. My thinking was that York was generally heaving with visitors, all on foot, and they were in town year-round. They were drawn by all sorts of attractions, among them the Yorvik Centre, the Railway Museum, Castle Museum, York Dungeon and so on. How hard would it be to add York Brewery to the list, thereby offering a bit of respite to some of the hard-pressed Dads, and relieving them of a bit of spare cash?

'Cash' was the operative word here. If we could get the punters up Toft Green and charge them to get in, maybe sell them a few odds and ends for coin of the realm, we'd be trotting along to the bank next day with a few of those dark blue bags in our sweaty hands. Much better than prising it from the tight fists of landlords, or waiting for wholesalers who seemed to think that three months was a perfectly acceptable time to sit on an invoice, no matter what it said in the terms of engagement. It would also ease our reliance on the factors at NatWest and the percentage they were creaming off.

I had no doubt that our tours were going to be a hit, and an instant hit at that. We'd had a few hundred leaflets printed, advertising tours at 12.30, 2.00, 3.30 and 5 p.m. We handed them out to a few youngsters, i.e., people who would work for 50 pence an hour, and sent them out to press them into the hands of likely-looking tourists. The charge? A modest £3 for adults, £2 for OAPs and Juniors (14-17), with kids free – so long as they were well supervised. What did they get for their money? A half-pint of Terrier, a half-pint of Stonewall and a half-hour of me, leading them around the brewery and brightening their day, with Smithy behind the bar rattling out the half-pints.

So, the first Saturday in July our brewery tours commenced. We'd shaved, we'd brushed our hair, put on our smartest jeans and York Brewery polo-shirts and were fully primed for this new venture into the tourist industry, which would begin with an invasion of camera-toting tourists, pockets full of money. It was only noon and I was already sweating. I'd written out my spiel several days previously, rehearsed it in front of the staff and survived their derision, then gone over all my jokes in front of the mirror at home. I was primed and ready. The question on my mind was, how the hell were we going to cope when the doors burst open and the first wave of visitors swarmed over the threshold? As the clock ticked towards a quarter past I went out onto Toft Green. I walked down to where I could see Rougier Street and the rows of weary tourists shuffling towards the City walls. It might have been a Saturday. It was a Saturday. So why weren't they heading my way? Well, it wasn't quite time, was it? Maybe they were all planning to show up at the last minute, or for one of the afternoon slots.

Back inside I went over my routine in my head. Taking the money, introducing myself, Smithy serving forty or fifty half-pints of Stonewall to get them started, then twenty minutes of yap while they ate a few crumbs of malted barley and rubbed the hops between their palms to savour its scent... Just long enough to acquaint them with the brewing process, short enough for them not to get bored. It was going to be a piece of cake. Later, as I got used to the tours I would sometimes manage six in a single day. Eventually I'd learn to get through the whole routine while thinking about totally unrelated matters – and the one occasion when I got caught out by a question I came back quick as a flash. 'The time to ask me questions is when you hear me say, 'Are there any questions?' Which of course I never did. That left them to fire their queries at Smithy, or whoever had the misfortune to serve them their halves of Yorkshire Terrier at the tour's end.

But that was a long way into the future. That first Saturday we drew a blank. Twelve-thirty came and went. I made a call to the guys we'd paid to hand out the leaflets. They had done it, hadn't they? Of course they had. Two o'clock passed, and three-thirty. Then five o'clock – our last chance. Not a sniff of a visitor. It was back to the drawing-board – or in this case to the Deramore Arms in Heslington to think it through on neutral territory.

The answer was obvious, really. We needed to put more effort – and cash - into sales and marketing, to put our name out there, along with news of the tours. We resolved that I would buy more leaflets, thousands of them this time. And we'd pay a company to distribute them – in pubs, hotels, guest-houses, information centres and so on.

It worked. It worked so well that before long I found I couldn't handle all the tours on my own and had to train up first Smithy, then Andrew, to stand in for me. The success of the new publicity campaign and the steady flow of visitors soon exposed a new problem that needed to be addressed. Not having a licence, we were unable to let our visitors buy beer. And that was a pity, because quite a few of them, after a tour, fancied hanging around and sinking a couple, before they called it a day. The two half-pints they got were part of the deal, but actual sales? All I could do was apologise and tell them it wasn't permitted. We did come up with one crafty little ruse whereby we sold them a beer mat and threw in a free pint, but we knew we mustn't push our luck.

What we needed was a liquor licence, and that required some thought. At the planning stage, remember, the police had opposed a licence on the grounds that Micklegate was well served by pubs and bars and was inclined to be a bit lively on an evening. I was pretty certain that, now that we'd been open a few months with no complaints, Arthur Swain, the police licensing officer, ought to be sympathetic to our case. So I suggested to him a restricted licence. Although our prime aim was to serve our tour customers a pint or two, we also wanted to get the general public into the bar. And so we came up with the idea of a Brewery Club.

When I met up with Arthur he was basically on my side, but told me he would run his eye over the Club's rules and regulations – and then they would go to the Licensing Magistrates for approval. The leader of this lot, the Chief Magistrate, was a wonderful old fellow named Alf Peacock, quite a character around York and a keen CAMRA supporter. Arthur arranged for him to visit the brewery on his own before the full committee came, in order that he might get a proper feel for what we were about.

Alf Peacock struck me as very astute. He asked intelligent questions and gave me the impression that he didn't suffer fools gladly, also that his opinion was probably going to be crucial. I came away pretty confident that he liked what he'd seen, was really taken with the brewing side of our operation and wanted to help us if he could. In fact, he gave me a few pointers – which I sensibly took as instructions – as to what we should include in our Club rules and regs in terms of the number of members, the cost of membership and our rules relating to guests. His final piece of advice was that we should go for an early closing time. That way we wouldn't pose any additional threat to the usual Micklegate mayhem.

A few days later I entertained the full magistrates' committee in the bar area. I treated them to my now standard tour lecture, then gave them a sample beer at the bar. I got them all to pick up a handful of hops, just as I did with all our visitors, persuaded them to rub it between their palms and inhale the aroma. As they all shuffled off to the toilet to wash away the yellow stain I had a good feeling. I'd engaged their interest in the process. This was going to happen. By the time I'd served them their second half-pint and apologised for the fact that, no matter how thirsty there were, I couldn't sell them another, I was pretty sure that I'd made my point.

I showed up at the Magistrates' Court in Clifford Street a week or two later and waited my turn. I waited all morning, went out for lunch during the adjournment, then resumed my seat and struggled to stay awake as one case after another was dealt with. Finally I heard the call for the York Brewery licence application. I had to go into a witness box, take the Good Book in my right hand and swear to God that I would speak the truth. I was then asked to tell the assembled judiciary – my pal Alf and two of his colleagues – exactly what I had in mind and why they should view my request favourably. I basically gave them the same spiel they'd heard at the brewery – without the jokes. They listened, nodded at each other and, upon hearing that the police had no objections, granted me my licence. This called for a drink…

In years to come I would be back several times to renew the licence, and it was gratifying to see how often a couple of the sitting magistrates would declare an interest and leave the bench. The reason? They were members of the Brewery Club. Talk about having friends in high places! In more recent times the entire procedure has changed. Magistrates are no longer involved, and it's the police and the council between them who make the decisions. It's all done through the post: much more efficient and convenient – but nowhere near as interesting.

Once the elation of having got a licence subsided we were left to confront an uncomfortable fact. We were free to sell beer until 9 p.m., but someone was going to have to stay behind and pull the pints. It soon became pretty obvious that it would fall to me and Smithy. We accepted our fate and decided that as far as was practical we would simply take it in turns. Neither of us was ablaze with excitement at the prospect of talking bollocks to a bunch of bar-flies after a hard day's graft, but it had to be done. You needed the patience of a saint to keep up the cheery banter with the odd club member – and some of them were very odd indeed – when you'd spent the day cleaning out the mash tun, washing casks, conducting brewery tours and selling beer.

There was Michael the Austrian who talked endlessly about whatever was on his mind – none of it remotely interesting – but killed us with kindness, always buying one more beer for himself and any other poor sod who was daft enough to engage in conversation with him. He would tell us over and over how important it was to support a new venture like ours, and always placed his money in the cash-tin with a theatrical flourish.

If Michael took a night off you could bet that he'd be replaced by resident hard man Harry. I knew he was a hard man, because the first time he came in he took me to one side to explain at great length that he had no need to prove himself these days. Just a glance from his steel-blue eyes, he confided, and any would-be trouble-maker would be stopped in his tracks, hypnotised by fear. Once in a while Michael and Harry, whose combined personalities were roughly that of an empty half-pint glass, would show up together. I often fantasised that the Austrian would insult our self-appointed keeper of the peace and never be seen again – then tried to imagine the dent that would make in our takings. Such musings whiled away many a tedious evening. Other times I would be distracted by the resident Lesbian couple, who enjoyed our beer almost as much as they enjoyed arguing with each other. I once tried to step in when they were on the point of fisticuffs. Big mistake. They rounded on me, and among the epithets that echoed down the alleyway as they stomped off into the night were 'uppity little brewery shit' and 'boring little straight guy'.

Perhaps I should have adopted the Smithy approach with these people. Being a Yorkshireman, he didn't try very hard to disguise his feelings. More than once I saw an unsuspecting punter approach the bar all bright-eyed and bushy tailed, only for 'mine host' to greet him with a stentorian 'What?' I tried to be more tactful, stifling a yawn every few minutes and praying that the last die-hard would sup up and bugger off home. Even so, I reminded myself that my heart was in this. I was the one who'd put a favourite quotation from the American writer and inventor Benjamin

Franklin on the back of our members' cards: 'Beer is the proof that God loves us and wants us to be happy.' And that was the point, really, that despite the oddities we attracted, our growing membership were united by that common love of good beer. And, when the place filled up, which it did more regularly now, there was a genuine atmosphere of bonhomie. It gave me great pleasure, as I wrote this, to see that Matt Moore, the excellent manager, and his team had won the York Club of the Year award for 2016 – although I wondered why it took CAMRA twenty years to recognise a place serving six hand-pulls of beer, freshly brewed on the premises and having room for eighty guests. Well, better late than never.

By this time I'd left my cosy little flat at the university. It was required by some damned academic. I'd moved out to Heworth and a poky ground-floor flat next door to the Walnut Tree pub. A young couple who were passionately in love and didn't care who knew it had the room above me. I didn't have many possessions in those days. Half my stuff had gone into storage. Phil Bell, another Heslington CC stalwart, accommodated the rest of it in his garage. I hung onto the kids' bunk beds so that I could accommodate the occasional visitor. It was all quite a contrast after having a view of the university lake, the willow trees, the waterfowl - and some gorgeous young female students walking by. The only halfway pleasant memory I have of Lilac Cottage was a lovely lady who worked behind the bar in the Walnut Tree. I made many futile attempts to chat her up. She was very sweet but it was quite clear that I didn't float her boat.

I was now within a mile or so of the brewery, but I still drove in to work every day in the faithful old Lada I'd bought when Little Chef took my company car from me.

One night in October 1997 I volunteered to drop off a couple of casks ordered by the Deramore Arms. Naturally enough, after I'd taken them to the cellar I had a bit a chin-wag with the landlord. Would I like a beer? Of course I would. It was good to see a few familiar faces, and of course everyone wanted to know how the new venture was going.

When closing time came I knew I really ought to have called a taxi, but as so many have done before me I thought, ah, it's not far, and the roads'll be nice and quiet. They were - and that meant the occupants of the police-car had little to occupy them when I drove past. They stopped me on Melrosegate, blue lights flashing. Two coppers got out. The first one told me I had a brake-light out. 'Oh, sorry,' I said, 'I'll get it fixed first thing in the morning.' Then the other one chimed in. 'And you were driving erratically.' 'Was I?' I asked. 'Yes. You nearly hit the sleeping policeman.'

That seemed ridiculous to me, and I didn't try to hide it. 'Everybody nearly hits them,' I said. 'If I'd been driving erratically I'd have clouted it.' They weren't in the mood for chit-chat. They invited me to take a seat in their car and a breath-test, which I failed. They took me to Fulford police station and asked me to blow three times into a machine. There was no reprieve. I remember sitting there, wondering whether I could afford a taxi, and how long it would take me to walk back to town and on to Heworth. I needn't have worried. They insisted on offering me a bed for the night.

I slept very well in my cell, and was awoken at six next morning by a copper bearing a very decent cup of tea. I walked into work – much to Smithy's amusement. I phoned Arthur Swain, the guy who'd helped me get the licence for the brewery club. When he'd stopped laughing I asked him what I could do to counteract the bad publicity I was attracting. He had a think and suggested I join their anti-drink-driving campaign, and of course I readily agreed.

That evening as I trudged home I passed a news vendor

and distinctly heard him shout something about a 'brewery boss'. I stopped, bought a paper, and there on page seven was my ugly mug and a report of my case.

Before I knew it I was in court. I was fined £400 and banned for eighteen months. The upside was that, in order to pay the fine, I finally got rid of the ugliest car ever to come out of Europe and bought myself the first new bike I'd ever possessed, although it wasn't long before that went missing – stolen from inside the brewery premises. And so I ended up walking in every day, which Smithy thought highly amusing. The first time he saw me plodding along Layerthorpe with my black woolly hat on, fists in my pockets, he said I 'looked like a bloody thug'.

I coped with the ban pretty well. I took the train to meetings, or got Smithy or one of the draymen to chauffeur me. The press now referred to me in all their write-ups as Tony 'Shanks's Pony' Thomson.

Far from being an impediment, the driving ban worked in our favour. With Richard taking over the deliveries, Smithy and I were now pretty well tied to the brewery premises, which was where we needed to be. Sales were growing and we were brewing more, but basically, we only had Nick and Andrew downstairs, and they still had to call on us to clean out the mash-tun. It was a two-and-a-half-hour job on a good day. The spent grain had to be dug out and loaded in a row of dustbins, which were collected after each brew by a local farmer and used as animal feed. After that we had to enter the vessel with buckets of caustic soda, lift off the heavy metal plates and scrub them down. Just when we thought we'd completed the job, along would come Andrew to inspect our work. Somehow he'd always find a section that wasn't up to scratch, and he had no hesitation in making us do it all over again.

The copper also needed to be cleaned out thoroughly

after every brew. The spent hops were collected by one of the gardeners at Castle Howard, thus forging a link which was to pay dividends in the future. When their Estate Manager, Duncan Peake, wanted a bottled beer to sell in their shop we were able to offer Brideshead Bitter, named after the massively popular BBC TV series which was filmed around the estate, *Brideshead Revisited*.

As well as seeing to all these mundane tasks, we starting spotting other areas where changes needed to be made. We had a pretty Heath Robinson arrangement for racking beer and it was resulting in a lot of waste. Some of the brews were particular lively and frothed over as we filled the casks, with the result that we often stood there watching perfectly good beer – and our profits – going down the drain. We were also aware that Steve, our unofficial quality controller, was taking his tasting duties a little too seriously, and was occasionally coming into work late and looking knackered before he even got started. Occupational hazards...

If it seems that we were over-concerned with cleanliness, consider this. As part of his contract with us, David Smith conducted four audits a year, taking a full day to inspect all areas of the premises. He only carried out his inspection when Andrew and Nick were brewing. He took swabs at every stage of the process, and sent them off to a laboratory in Sunderland, Brewlab, for analysis. A couple of weeks later we'd receive a report. The first time I tried to read one I realised it was way over my head, what with all the microbiological and chemical terms. I called Andrew into the office and asked him to help me decode it. We went through it page by page, then arrived at the section that measured the actual condition of the finished beer – and any bacteria lurking within it. The letters 'TNTC' appeared – not once but several times. 'What's that mean?' I asked. Andrew's reply was to the effect that nobody ever got ill by drinking beer, and that if bacteria are present the alcohol will kill most of them – certainly enough to render it safe. 'Yeah,' I said, 'but what do the letters stand for?' 'You don't want to know,' he said. 'But I do.' Finally I got it out of him. 'Look,' he said, 'there's nothing to worry about.' Then he lowered his eyes and said, 'It stands for... Too Numerous To Count.'

Clearly, as thorough as we'd tried to be, we weren't getting the cleaning right. We reviewed our procedures immediately, and that was the last time that dreaded collection of letters appeared on one of David's reports.

Part of my grand scheme for the brewery had always been the club bar, but we soon realised that it wasn't going to become a hot-spot for revellers unless we took action.

In those early days it was in danger of becoming a haven for the friendless, the beer-obsessed and the charismatically challenged. Working the bar at night was pure torment. Some nights we'd have barely a handful of customers – on one or two occasions none at all. We took to playing bagatelle – and roping in any stray drinker who drifted in. Eventually we got to hear that a woman we both knew, liked and respected, a former colleague at Little Chef who'd been a top-notch branch manager for many years, had finished with them. Any chance she'd fancy a nice part-time job? Smithy in particular had had a close working relationship with Barbara Vincent, who lived down the A64 in the brewing town of Tadcaster. He talked her into joining us part-time, running the bar and conducting tours.

The fact is that in those early days the brewery dominated our lives. No question about that. However, Smithy and I did have time off, and each of us did have some kind of a private life. I'd never given much thought to what my partner was up to on his rare days off, but one evening, after a long hard shift, he invited me into the bar and told me we needed to talk. 'I've something to tell you,' he said. 'You'd best sit down. I'll pour you a drink. Trust me, you'll bloody want it when you've heard this.'

When it came to investment, brewing process was always top of the list...

At that moment, as I pulled out a bar stool, I braced myself. I was certain I knew what was coming. The long hours, lousy pay, the failure to set the world alight. It had all got too much, and my partner was jumping ship. 'Go on.' I said, 'let's have it.'

'I'm out,' he said. 'Yep.' I nodded my head wearily. I was right. 'Aye,' he continued, 'I've decided it's time to stop bloody pretending and come out. I'm gay.' He was looking at me as if awaiting disapproval, condemnation, abuse. I laughed aloud. 'Is that it? Is that your news?' 'Well, yes,' he said. 'I've been building up to this for bloody long enough. So what are you saying, you're okay with it?' 'Okay?' I said. 'You're lucky I didn't kiss you. I thought you were about to sling your hook.' 'You what?' he said. 'Never. This is our business, our livelihood, our future.' So there we were, alone in the bar, celebrating his new identity as an 'out' gay man, and he was telling me about the partner he'd met – and with whom he was going to share a house, and his life.

There was an amusing 'P.S.' to this revelation a little while later. We had a young research student from York University working for us as a part-time tour guide. On one of our staff nights out Smithy had a few drinks and said to her, 'You know I'm gay? And I've come out?' Unfazed, Celina replied, 'That's no surprise. We'd all figured that out. Now I'll tell you something you don't know.' 'Oh,' says Smithy, 'and what's that?' 'I'm shagging your head brewer.'

Celina was that kind of character: straightforward and outspoken. She took no crap from anybody. One day, conducting a party of thirty or so around the brewery, she had one visitor who kept asking ever more searching questions, clearly trying to stump her. He really shouldn't have bothered. Celina was a very bright young woman. She had a degree in Chemistry, and what she didn't know about yeast was hardly worth knowing. She waited until they stopped to look through the window into the fermenting room. Below them the yeast bubbled and seethed, and everybody agreed it was an impressive sight. When Mister Smart-Arse raised yet another query, Celina let him have it. She launched into a lecture on microbiological organisms, throwing in every arcane, polysyllabic term she could come up with – which was quite a few. When it was plain that the guy was ready to sue for peace she smiled sweetly – and the rest of the party grinned broadly as she asked, 'Does that make sense now?'

I should add, to save any blushes, that Andrew and Celina have been happily married for quite a few years now.

Around the time of Smithy's bold announcement I had the good fortune to meet the woman who was later to become my second wife. I was back at the magistrates' court on licensing business. The place was even more crowded than usual so I went and found myself a seat in the corridor – right alongside a very attractive blonde-haired lady who had her head buried in a book. When I stole a glance at her face I was pretty sure I'd actually seen her in our bar. I remember thinking, well, I'm not going to pass up an opportunity like this, so I introduced myself. 'Hi,' I said, 'I'm Tony Thomson from York Brewery. I've got a feeling we may have met.'

'Yes,' she replied, 'I've been there. I bought a baseball cap to go running in.' And then she carried on reading. I thought I'd blown it, and went outside to have a consoling cigarette – although later she would tell me she thought I was very ill-mannered, taking myself off for a fag when I could've stayed and chatted with her. She was wrong on that, but dead right when she told me I didn't understand women.

It turned out that I hadn't blown it entirely. A few days later I got a call from her. She introduced herself as Julie Mett and told me she was on the Ladies Licensed Victuallers' Association dinner-dance committee. Was I intending to go? I'd never heard of it, but of course I was all ears now. 'Yeah,' I told her. 'I'd love to. Only trouble is, I've nobody to go with.'

'That's okay,' she said. 'I haven't either. We can go together. It's at the race-course.'

When the night of the ball came around she picked me up in a taxi – at the brewery. Where else? I was never away from the place. I remember I was in the bar, huffing and puffing and wishing I'd taken Smithy's advice and bought one of those bow-ties with an elastic band that just clip on your shirt-collar. I nearly choked when she walked in, drop-dead gorgeous and all done up in her finery. There were a few members in the bar comparing notes on the latest brew, but she stopped them all in their tracks. They sat there, mouths open, while Julie re-arranged my tie out with a deft movement of her fingers, took my arm and escorted me out into the night.

Our romance had a few obstacles to overcome. Not the least was her boyfriend in the United States. She made no secret of his existence, and frequently took off on transatlantic jaunts, leaving me to cope with the fact that for the moment I was, as she liked to remind me, only her 'designated U.K. shag'.

13.
BREWERY? BREWERY? YOU WANT TO BE IN TADCASTER, LAD.

Our leaflet raid on the city produced results. The tour numbers were increasing month by month. What was interesting was the number of times we heard someone say, 'We never realised you were here.' It was always the same: they'd ask a copper, or a traffic warden or some local and get the same answer, every time. 'Brewery? Nah, you want to be in Tadcaster, lad. There's no brewery in York.' When they were showed the leaflet it was, 'Well, I'll be blowed.'

After hearing the same tale week after week I began to wonder whether I could get something more permanent than leaflets, something to put us on the map. There are a number of handsome metal posts around the city – like old-fashioned lamp standards, with signs on them pointing passers-by to the Railway Museum, the Minster, the Viking Centre and so on. What if we could get a sign directing them to Toft Green?

I called the City Council, and was told that we certainly qualified as an attraction that might be included on the list –

providing there was adequate space on the posts. I can't recall how many went up, but I seem to remember ordering ten and only being invoiced for two, albeit at £100 a throw.

At the beginning, the bar was a simple enough set-up: a few tables and chairs, and precious few adornments. But as we got into the spirit of the thing we started to give it a bit more of a pub character. I introduced a 'yard of ale' glass. The idea was that people would challenge each other to drink its contents (three pints) in one go. Many tried, and all ended up spluttering to an unsatisfactory conclusion. Then one night we got a hen party in. Daft frocks, suspender belts, acres of bare flesh and the now statutory giant inflatable dildo. 'Yard of ale?' one of them said. 'Give it to our Kylie.' I filled the vessel, and watched as the girls' appointed champion raised it to her lips, threw her head back and disposed of the lot. She stood there for a moment, swaying slightly, then headed for the toilet. We couldn't rely on others being so reliable or lady-like – and soon learned to place a galvanised iron bucket next to the contestant.

It would be some time before we extended the bar area,

making room for as many as eighty guests, and installing another toilet. Until then we managed with one. We did get the odd comment about not having dedicated ladies and gents, but answered with, 'We want you to feel at home here – and you don't have signs on the door at home, do you?'

Now that we were getting into our stride we felt confident enough to engage with the public in a more relaxed way. It was hot work for Andrew and Nick, down in the brew-house, and they started stripping off their shirts and T-shirts. Then they took to wearing shorts. They were young, fit lads back then and can't have been oblivious to the admiring glances they got from some of our female visitors. Andrew enjoyed disrupting the tours. Often, when he heard one of us making some vague statement about the brewing process, he would shout out, 'Don't listen to him. He hasn't a clue!' Or he'd just shout out 'Wrong!' at the top of his voice.

Leading the tours was repetitive, and we rotated the job as much as possible. I roped in my eldest daughter, Tessa, during her summer vacation from university. She needed the money, and I was glad of a break.

With Barbara behind the bar most nights, Smithy and I now had time for a social life. We were both courting. I was seeing more of Julie, and he had met the man who was to be his life partner, a charming surgeon and excellent raconteur called Trevor. Among the regulars in the club was a fellow called Mick Waite. I knew him as a team-mate at Heslington C.C. He'd been made redundant around this time, and to add to his woes his wife had left him – which probably accounted for his turning up at the club rather more often. He loved the place, relished the beer, and showed up night after night. He was almost, but not quite, in the same league as legendary member Ray Roberts. Ray had been shoe-horned out of his job and forced to retire from British Rail, with whom he had spent all his working life. His speciality was timetables, and how to draw them up. His old office was barely two minutes' walk away. He hadn't been retired long when they realised they couldn't manage without him and asked him to return. He always sat on 'Ray's stool', which was right beside the Brewery Club Members' notice board, perfectly positioned for him to keep an eye on it, review it, approve or disapprove of the notices and articles that were posted on it. He seemed so much a part of the place that I officially appointed him Brewery Club Liaison Officer, a role in which he excelled. He filtered all the comments, only passing on to me such feedback as he thought worthy of our consideration. He really did save me a lot of the hassle of dealing with the more idiosyncratic members who had an axe to grind. I was on holiday when he died in 2014 and was upset at missing his funeral. There was, I heard, a particularly fine eulogy from Sam Moss, a former barman at the Club who had by this time set up the Leeds Brewery in partnership with Michael Brothwell. After the funeral they saw Ray off – not with his favourite Terrier, but with a special beer called Cheers Ray! Ale.

Sam and Michael had been fellow students at York University. Both had worked behind our bar and conducted tours, which was how they got to know Ray so well. They were a couple of very bright lads, determined to set up their own brewery. Being very young, however, they couldn't find a bank to help them – unless they could find a couple of backers with a track record in the industry. Smithy and I fully believed that they had what it took to do well and offered our support. They set up Leeds Brewery in 2007 and have never looked back, opening a number of pubs in Leeds and two in York. We were well rewarded for our investment, Smithy selling his shares in 2015 while I chose to retain mine. I still take the train over to Leeds to visit the lads, especially when they're looking for another pub to open. It's a great excuse to sample a few of their superb ales. The only problem has been staying awake on the way back to York – as I realised the day I woke up and saw that we were pulling into Darlington.

Mick Waite also found a permanent role at the Club. After seeing his face night after night, and seeing how well he engaged with strangers who came in, I asked him if he fancied working behind the bar and being trained up to lead the tours. He nearly bit my hand off, and took to the job like a duck to water. But then he would. He'd been born in the John Bull pub in Layerthorpe, where his parents were the licensees. When his Dad died he'd been sent away to board at a school for the sons and daughters of licensed victuallers down in Slough. More recently he'd converted part of his house into a mini pub with two hand-pulls.

Mick loved his work. He chatted with the tourists as he showed them around the place, and would happily sit and talk with them afterwards in the bar. He stayed with us for thirteen years, racking up, by his own reckoning, over 6,000 tours. He loved numbers, and would rattle them off. Not content to tell the punters that each brew made 20 barrels at 36 gallons apiece, or 5,760 pints, he would throw in the fact that a man (or woman) who consumed a modest four pints a day would take four years to drink the place dry. By the time Mick retired we were cranking out ten brews and he'd had to update his figures several times. No problem for a guy who had counted how many steps he took in walking from his house to the brewery – it was 1,866 – and was concerned, a year later, to find it had increased to 1,878. He so enjoyed the visiting stag and hen parties that came in at the weekend that he went eight years without ever having a Saturday off. He was organised too. If he started a tour at three o'clock, he'd count the numbers then tell the barman, 'At twenty-five past I want you to pull thirty-six halves of Terrier – and at three-thirty on the dot he'd bring the punters back for the second instalment of their refreshment.

Mick was a many-faceted individual. He was a keen painter who found time to turn out some terrific paintings – many of them cricket scenes. He sold one of them to the legendary commentator Christopher Martin-Jenkins. Later on, as manager of the bar and visitor centre, he recruited a succession of first-year students to work with us, youngsters who would come back every year until they graduated. In retirement he still gets Christmas cards from many of them.

Club membership grew steadily from those early beginnings. Next door to us was a barristers' chambers, home to thirty or so legal eagles and their support team. I offered them a corporate deal whereby the whole firm could be signed up at reduced rates. The barristers joined en bloc – although the good news was tempered by their request that we started stocking some decent wines, not a subject I knew much about. They certainly elevated the tone of the bar-room chat, however, and I would often listen with interest as they discussed the various cases they were working on. They also dispensed advice when it was required – as when I had to appear in court over a wholesaler who owed us for £2,000-worth of bottled beer. I was briefed, in detail, as to what I should or should not say. I was so confident that by the time I was called to state my case I was actually looking forward to it. Sadly, the guy I was suing failed to appear. When the bailiffs eventually went to his house they found nothing of value – and we had to roll with a £2,000 loss.

As the brewery tours gained in popularity and club membership increased, it became obvious that we needed to expand the accommodation for our visitors. Beyond the bar area were two further rooms, as yet unused. I reckoned that if we could expand into them we would create a space for as many as eighty guests, as well as a small retail area where we could sell gift-packs of beer, mugs, glasses and suchlike. We could also extend the actual bar, install a couple more hand-pumps and offer punters – I shuddered at the very thought – a choice of lagers. Once we'd made those changes, we would be able to advertise for party nights with a buffet included.

Among the long list of membership rules we'd established was one which permitted each member to have one party night per year, to which they could invite their friends, members or not. This would all be good for cash-flow and general turnover, not to mention sales of beer. Mister Grumpy at our solicitors had by this time moved on. His replacement, Sally Robinson, was a rarity in that world, being highly efficient, extremely intelligent – she'd been educated at Cambridge – and possessed a great sense of humour, one which seemed to strike the right chord with Smithy. Sally now saw us through our dealings with our tenants and our superior landlord, Mr Donald Oliver.

The tours continued to grow in popularity. Through the York Tourist Board we started to receive parties of French school-children – older ones, aged 14-18. There would generally be a coach-load comprising around fifty of them plus five or six teachers. I never understood why they came, until someone explained to me that they'd been barred from most of York's attractions, for nicking stuff. They were a massive headache. After one tour I noticed that a whole lot of pots, ash-trays, glasses, pens, badges and lighters had disappeared from our display of items for sale. 'The thieving little buggers!' I shouted, and set off after them. I knew where to look: their teacher had already told me that their next stop was the Viking Centre on Coppergate.

I ran all the way, arriving breathless to find them

making their way through the entrance. When the teachers heard what I had to say they were aghast. Surely I wasn't accusing their fresh-faced innocents of… theft? I told them I was, and that if they didn't consent to have the kids' bags searched I'd call the cops. With classic French reluctance, the teachers pulled one of their little angels aside and got him to open his back-pack. Out came a pen, a mug and an ash-tray. By the time they'd gone through the lot I'd filled two plastic bags with assorted gifts they'd half-inched and left their red-faced teachers to sort out a suitable punishment.

I wasn't the only one who had trouble with our friends from across the Channel. When Andrew had an awkward gent on his tour he explained that the hops were a close relative of cannabis sativa and was gratified, an hour later, to find in the alleyway two or three discarded roll-ups stuffed full of hops – and a little pool of regurgitated lunch.

York thrives on its tourist business, of course, but some people find the influx of foreigners a bit of a challenge. I was told by the legendary manager of the Snickleway pub, Frank Cartin, that he'd made a special effort to foster his foreign relations. 'Oh,' I asked him, 'and what's that?' 'I've learned how to say fuck off in fifteen different languages.'

Frank was quite a character, and a very successful host. He had a happy knack of joining a group of customers just as they were getting to the end of their drinks and engaging in conversation with them. He always had a story, and he invariably seduced them into buying one more round. In fact, he would at times be involved in rounds at three or four separate tables. And the guy could put away beer. He once entertained a Pennsylvania D.A who claimed he could drink any Limey under the table. A few hours later he was out cold and Frank had to help put him and his friend to bed.

As our production increased we became ever more conscious of the fact that we had a lousy water supply. You need six pints of water to make a pint of beer – and an awful lot more to carry out the hygiene routines which are part and parcel of good brewing practice. Remarkably, the Toft Green premises had no mains water supply of its own. We got ours from the Pizzaland restaurant on Micklegate, which reached us via 150 feet of half-inch pipe – just about adequate when we were brewing once or twice a week, but absolutely hopeless now that we were getting busier.

When Pizzaland were going full bore our pressure would drop to a pathetic level. Filling a 20-barrel liquor tank, which required 720 gallons of water, could take half a day. We eased the problem slightly by installing a large storage tank in the roof space. That gave us some respite, but was never going to be the long-term solution. Then Pizzaland closed down, and our pressure went up. Fine, but sooner or later some business or other would move in and we'd be back where we started. With that in mind, we approached the water company and got them to create a new mains supply direct to us. This was great. There was, unfortunately, a down-side. For the first time we started getting bills for our water consumption. It was only then that we realised what had been going on – namely, that our consumption had all been recorded on the Pizzaland meter. Perhaps this is the moment to offer a belated 'thank you' to whoever paid the bill. You kept us in business in that tricky first year.

With the water supply sorted, we now concentrated on the extensions to the bar and hospitality areas. There was only one objection when we submitted our planning application, from a neighbour who actually lived in a house behind us – and that was put aside. I hired Regency Design, the Doncaster firm which had done our original building work. I didn't ask them for an estimate I simply told them how much I had to spend – namely, everything we had in the bank, which added up to £8,000. Their man Paul came and looked at the job, listened as I told him the extent of my available cash, and agreed to take it on. His lads did a great job. No complaints there – just that when I opened the envelope containing his invoice I saw that he was billing us for £14,000. I reminded him what we'd agreed, and he suggested we settle for £12,000. At that price, he insisted, he would get nothing out of the contract. I didn't have £12,000 available, and told him so. He ended up taking me to court, where the judge pointed out that we were both at fault for not putting our agreement in writing. We had little choice but to split the difference, meaning that I had to scrape around for a further £2,000. I must admit that I felt I'd been stitched up, and we never used the firm again. However, I'd learned a valuable lesson, one to bear in mind when we got tenders in for future work on our pubs.

Around this time we had a couple of staff changes. Stevie, our cask-washer, beer-racker and unofficial quality controller, told us he was moving on. Wraggy had been chewing my ear for some time about a young lad called Gary Curtis who, he assured us, would be an ideal recruit. We took him on and he gave us several years' sterling service – even though he was given one of the lousiest jobs in the place, shovelling out the mash tun after the completion of a brew. Gary was young, and not exactly worldly wise – neither was he, at the outset, the swiftest worker. Indeed, our esteemed Head Brewer was so exasperated by Gary's deliberate approach to his work that he ended up grabbing his ankles and holding him head down from the gallery, threatening to drop him in the mash-tun if he didn't speed up. Fortunately for Gary, we'd recently taken on a brewery assistant who still works at Toft Green, Steve Prior. It was Steve's idea to devise a more humane method of persuading Gary to pull his finger out. He convinced that lad that this was the job to make a man of him – to build up his muscles and make him irresistible to the opposite sex. With the aid of a stop-watch, a few shouts of encouragement, and a tape-recorder blasting out the Rocky theme at about 120 decibels, Steve got him up to speed. The mash tun was emptied in record time, Gary's physique shaped up nicely, and, in time, the lad found true love.

Many of the younger people we took on needed a little... guidance. William Roberts, who later joined us as a brewery assistant – which meant he got any job that nobody else felt like taking on – came to us a dedicated lager drinker, and that set us the challenge of educating his palate. Wills soon earned himself an unfortunate reputation. He found the environment warm, and the nature of his work – cleaning, racking, digging out the mash tun – meant that he was always sweating like a pig. That's when he discovered that the conditioning tanks were deliciously cool, and wrapped his arms around them in a loving embrace. A club member, glancing into the conditioning room, immediately christened him 'Tank Hugger'.

Before giving the go-ahead to builders always get quotes on a firm specification...

Nick and Andrew, meanwhile, were determined to get their new recruit drinking proper beer. They did get him to sample the odd glass of Guzzler, but the one that converted him was a single hop beer we brewed called SAAZ. It was based on hops from the Czech Republic – the same as was used in his favourite lager, Budvar, also Czech. Around this time he started dating a girl called Lucia, who came from

Prague. After Wills' conversion we deemed him fit to work behind the bar and conduct the tours, from where he graduated to a job in the Last Drop Inn, our first pub. His final move was to the brewery warehouse in The Crescent. He fully embraced the life of the brewery, even to turning out in a football team when we were challenged by the barristers next door. It was quite a sight, all these brain-boxes on one side, us on the other, with Smithy and Trevor on the touchline doing a fair imitation of Brian Clough and Peter Taylor as they shouted derogatory remarks.

I played in that game, and the two that followed, the lads having decided this was to be a best-of-three event. I survived the experience; I was still staying pretty fit. My daily round still included a healthy dose of physical work in the brewery. I was also having a lunchtime game of squash with my cricket buddy, Mike Shirley, two or three times a week. Too busy to be ill, I was telling everyone. It took some time for me to notice that I wasn't feeling right, and when I finally visited my local surgery I learned I had pleurisy, and was lucky that it hadn't developed into full-blown pneumonia.

But by now, when one of us had to have a bit of time off, the business could manage. As well as the full-time staff, we also started to take on students for two- to three-week work experience placements from Brew Lab in Sunderland. One by one we trained them in the delightful tasks of cask-washing and racking and were able to call on them whenever we needed extra help. Carol, our sales queen, had left by this time. She'd done a great job, but I suppose she had taken it as far as she could. The time was ripe to take on someone with a rather more refined sales technique. One of the benefits of going around town from pub to pub, trying to sell our beer, was that I got to know a lot of local characters. Among them was a woman called Sharon Nichols, Shaz to her mates. She was quite an artist, and had carved out a small niche for herself, chalking up menus and other advertisements on the blackboards that were now more and more common outside pubs and restaurants. She struck me as a real character with a great personality and a sharp wit. She also liked a pint. I thought she'd fit in nicely at our place, so I made her an offer and there she was, installed in the sales chair in Andrew's old office.

Shaz got a large road-map and marked out those areas of the country which our drivers could cover in a single day. Then she went through the *Good Beer Guide* and set about phoning all the pubs in those areas, the aim being to get enough orders to make a day-long trip worthwhile. The rust-bucket could carry, at a pinch, two dozen firkins, and by our reckoning an order amounting to twenty, at a profit of about £25 apiece, would make it worth our while. It was a rough calculation, because the price of a firkin wasn't fixed; it depended upon the ABV of the brew and how much duty was therefore payable. And of course it all depended on Shaz getting enough customers. We figured that we could cover all these areas we'd mapped out every six to eight weeks. By now we had set up ten routes, such as East Coast (north), Leeds, Derby, Nottingham and Lincolnshire, and so on. Plus Essex, of course. They varied in the amount of trade they gave us, but it meant that Shaz could focus more closely on the pubs within each area, rather than picking up random orders that didn't suit our planned routes. It also meant that we were now sending the van out with a decent load, rather than travelling huge distances to satisfy a handful of orders.

As things progressed, and as our reputation grew – both for the reliability of our product and our ability to complete orders on time – we would have to hire a second van from time to time and take on a part-time drayman. The man we hired was Keith Nelson, a real grafter who would soon be taken on full-time and stay with us for several years. Keith hadn't been with us very long when I became convinced that we might have to let him go. Reports were reaching my ears that the York Brewery van, emblazoned with our name on its front, back and sides, was frequently to be seen parked

outside a local betting shop. Was he skiving off to have a crafty bet on the 3.20 at Fakenham? It turned out that, much as Keith enjoyed a flutter, he wasn't taking us for ride. He happened to have rented a flat above the bookies. Although we'd found our feet we still managed to collect on our client list what you'd call characterful landlords – or, as Smithy referred to them, 'bloody tossers'. There was a fellow in the Stockport area of Greater Manchester who regularly rubbed us up the wrong way. I'd had a particularly difficult day when he called me, in the middle of the afternoon, to complain that our drayman had dropped a nine-gallon cask at the cellar door, then driven off and left it. I told him Richard had left the yard very early in the morning as he had a long round to complete, that he hadn't been able to raise the landlord from his slumbers and therefore decided to do the sensible thing and leave the cask in a convenient place. The landlord listened to what I was saying, then said, 'Aye, but I've got a broken arm, me. I can't do it. When's he coming back to drop it in the cellar?' Somehow managing to maintain my pleasant and polite tone, I gritted my teeth and said, 'He isn't. He has a long list of pubs to deliver to and by the time he's finished he'll be the other side of Manchester on his way back to York. Can't you get one of your bar staff to do it? Or one of your regulars?'

There was a moment's silence, after which the landlord said, 'I'm not asking my customers to lug a bloody cask down them steps. That's your job.' 'Okay,' I said, 'let me have a think and I'll get back to you.' I rang off, sat back in my seat and had a cigarette. When I'd calmed down I called the guy back. 'Don't worry,' I said, 'I've worked it out.' 'Oh, good,' he said. 'Yeah, I've got this mate who owes me one. He lives in Paris. I've had a word and what we'll do is, we'll fly him over to Manchester, call him a taxi and he'll drop your cask into the cellar for you. If his plane's on time he should be with you around midday tomorrow. That okay?' There was a long silence. Then he said, 'I don't think there's any need for that.' 'No,' I said, 'and no need for you to worry yourself. It'll be picked it up tomorrow – and we won't bother you again.' It was as Smithy liked to say: some of them needed telling.

Awkward sods were one thing, but some landlords were just plain nasty. We had one in a village pub on the outskirts of York. He'd had beer off us, failed to pay, and when we made enquiries we heard that the place had shut down. Smithy decided to go and sort it out – or at least collect our empty casks. When he got there he found the landlord still on the premises, very aggressive and threatening. Smithy gathered up the empty casks from around the back and beat a retreat. As he drove off he heard a lot of banging and pinging. He looked in the wing-mirror, and there was the landlord hurling stones at him.

In business you never know when the next break is around the corner. I'd got to know a very engaging fellow called Dave Aucett who ran a wholesaler called East West Ales. Among the chains he supplied was Wetherspoons, and he managed to negotiate me a great deal with them – not so much in terms of our initial order, rather in terms of our profile. What he did was to get our beers into their pubs for two slots of three months each. That meant that for six months of the year our pump-clips – and our beer – would be in one of the fastest-growing pub chains in the country.

Of course, Dave didn't work this one just so that he could put money into our bank account. He wanted his slice. A big fat slice. The guy drove a hard bargain, which basically consisted of him telling me what price he was willing to pay me. In his eyes, that was it. Deal done. My response was, 'That's insane. You're not the only one who has to make a profit, you know. Look, I'll sleep on it. Call you tomorrow.'

It's called postponing the evil day. Next morning I took a deep breath and got on the phone. He knew what was coming. He could probably recite it by heart, because he'd had this sort of wrangle more than once. 'Look, Dave, we're a city centre show brewery. We pay high rates. We've invested a lot of money in equipment that other breweries don't have – just to ensure a consistently high quality product.' All this time, naturally enough, I was hoping he'd interrupt me and go, yeah, sure, fair point, and revise his price upwards. But no, not a peep from the other end of the phone. 'I mean, we're paying for both our brewers to study for their industry qualifications. That's how much we care. And it's the reason why we never let you down. So, all in all' – even as I finished my spiel I could feel the wind going out of my sails – 'all in all, mate, I reckon we're worth a few extra quid.' At which point I'd name my price. In fact, he always agreed to adjust his offer in our favour. Not a lot, but enough to make me feel I'd won a victory of sorts. But I'm not sure I had. He enjoyed the whole process. To settle matters at a first discussion would have robbed him of the thing he liked, a bit of old-fashioned haggling.

It's worth talking about Wetherspoons. A lot of people are suspicious of them, perhaps even a bit sniffy. 'Oh yeah, Wetherspoons,' they'll tell you, 'they can sell it cheap because it's coming up to its sell-by date. Nobody else wants it.' Not true. If the beer didn't have at least three weeks 'best-before' on it, David would turn it down flat. As to keeping prices so low, that was a two-way street between the chain wanting to undercut the opposition, and the brewery wanting to shift large volumes of beer. We were happy with that. As we saw it, the size of their orders entitled them to a good discount.

We were now dealing with most leading wholesalers in the UK and showing them that we could always provide first-rate beer on schedule. However, we were still plagued by our old nemesis, the cask shortage. The plastic ones were keeping us going but we knew they weren't the long-term solution, and we were starting to track down offers on the stainless steel variety. Every time I heard of another brewery closing down I'd be on the phone, asking whether they had any they wanted to unload. Slowly but surely, we built up our stock. Cheap as these cast-offs were, we still had to fork out on re-branding and re-numbering them.

All our profit was thus being re-invested. It's what any growing business must do, but of course it didn't help our cash-flow. Some years later a fellow businessman said to me, 'You did it the hard way, Tony. The easy way would be to buy up an estate of eight or ten pubs, then set up a brewery with a ready market.' The guy was dead right, not that I realised it when I set out on the project. Besides, there was finance to consider. Pubs aren't cheap – and you need to pay people to run them. However, at the back of my mind was always the intention to get into the pub business.

Thanks to our angel at Nurdin & Peacock we were in a position to arrange for a second bottling run with Robinsons pretty soon after the first. A run would consist of a 50-barrel brew yielding roughly 1300 cases or 15,600 bottles, each case consisting of 12 x 500ml bottles. The costs worked out at £9,000, or £7 a case, as near as makes no difference. It's worth noting that 40 per cent of the outlay was for beer duty.

Once we'd sent a brew off to Robinsons we had to make sure we were ready to receive the return load. Sixteen pallets take some storing. We allocated the first two store-rooms up the alleyway by the entrance to the brewery – the ones we'd managed to take over by default – and hoped they would take the first consignment, which arrived on the back of not one, but two, very large lorries. We were ready. We'd hired a fork-lift truck for a set time, and a driver. He managed to get all the pallets off the trucks easily enough, then revealed a weakness in his spatial awareness – or, to put it more bluntly, the driving skills of a five-year-old on the dodgems. How he didn't break half the bottles I'll never know, but there was a lot of bumping and crashing and a good deal of industrial language as he proceeded to dump half the pallets in the yard, the other half on the road outside. It was at this juncture that he announced his time was up. We'd had our two hours or whatever it was and he had to go back to base.

So there we were, Smithy and I, Andrew, Nick and Gary, looking at sixteen pallets, each containing eighty cases of beer. How the hell were we going to fit them all into our two store-rooms? The answer was, we weren't. And in any case, we had the more pressing task of manhandling them to a secure location. You don't go leaving a stack of beer in the street in the best of circumstances, and certainly not in the vicinity of the Micklegate run.

We formed a human chain and started passing the cases hand to hand into the storage area. And somehow it grew. First it was the five of us, one at the pallet, one at the store entrance, the others lugging the cases several yards and staggering back to grab the next one. Then a couple of guys who'd booked a tour and turned up early volunteered. Two club members who'd dropped in for a beer, they joined in too. We even enticed a passer-by or two with the offer of a free case of beer. Before we knew it we were turning willing helpers away. From Mission Impossible we were soon closing in on Mission Accomplished.

Back in the bar, cooling down with a few hard-earned pints, we agreed that it had been a truly epic endeavour, the stuff of legends, but it had also been bloody hard work. We couldn't afford a repeat performance. I was recommended another fork-lift driver, a chap called Philip Atkinson who had his own business. This guy should have entered the world fork-lift drivers' championship. He would have been a serious contender. The way he got those pallets off the lorry, turned on the proverbial sixpence, and dropped them into the tightest spaces was sheer poetry. Apart from showering him with praise, we always offered him a few beers to take home, which he gratefully accepted.

The good news, however, was that we had risked the bottled beer option, and gained a further improvement in sales – especially locally. Getting pubs to take the cask ales had been tough. By contrast, we had a much easier time with restaurants, cafés, hotels, off-licences and so on. Shaz was

using her local knowledge and contacts to find new outlets, many of which were effectively run by individuals who were free to make a quick decision and buy in whatever suited them. They weren't having to ring some suit at Head Office. This was doubly helpful to us in that it brought our product to people's notice, and helped put us on the map.

As ever, there were downs as well as ups. One day, around noon, I received a visitor at the brewery, a Canadian guy called Frank. He breezed in off the street and demanded to speak to the Managing Director – immediately, he said, as he was in the market for beer. Lots of it.

It's hard not to get excited when faced with someone who's threatening to buy up your entire current stock, but I did my best to stay calm. We sat in the bar and he lectured me on what a terrific guy he was and how, if I played my cards right, I would land an order for a massive quantity of beer. He showed me his card, which said he was the owner of a wholesale operation in Toronto. I gave him a quick tour. He looked at his watch and suggested that since I was going to make a pile of money from him I might take him to lunch at the best restaurant in town. I wouldn't say the alarm was ringing yet, but the bell-ringers were certainly spitting in their hands, ready to pull on the ropes. And I was coming to the conclusion that this guy was a total prick. I told him I was too busy to go out to lunch and added that I'd already shoved a long list of jobs to one side to accommodate him. I also pointed out that he should have made an appointment. But, just in case he might be genuine, I promised to treat him to a slap-up meal – when or if a life-changing order arrived.

Frank had been a nuisance from the moment he stepped in off Toft Green, and remained a nuisance for some time to come. After he'd gone home he continued to phone from across the Atlantic, talking about massive orders. He even got me to agree to re-labelling Yorkshire Terrier as Minster Ale for him – and unwittingly did me a favour. 'Nobody in Canada gives a shit about a little old dog,' he told me, 'but they're sure as hell impressed with that church.'

I pointed out that I'd have to get a label designed – which would not be cheap – and that I'd have to get Robinsons to swap the labels in the middle of their bottling run, which would be inconvenient. As it happened, the design I commissioned would later win an award as the best label of the year – but that was in the future. Right now this fellow was seriously pissing me off.

Finally, one afternoon, Frank called from Toronto to say I could expect his order within a couple of hours, by fax. So I was wrong, after all. The pillock was actually going to deliver on his airy promises. I almost felt guilty for all the bad things I'd thought and said about him over the past few weeks.

To be fair to this guy, he had spelled out to me in some

detail the way that beer was exported to Canada. It took some believing. When he, as a bona fide wholesaler, put in an order he made it via the Canadian Customs and Excise people. They would check the details and, with luck and a following wind, agree to it. The actual order would then come, not from the wholesaler, but from the relevant Government department. The brewer would ship out the beer to a bonded warehouse. Upon its arrival Customs would check it over, then inform the wholesaler that they could come and get it – but only after they'd paid Customs and Excise the amount on the invoice. Upon receipt of that, the Government would pay the supplier – in this case, York Brewery.

I suggested to Frank that it was a procedure worthy of some eastern European state, and that it could only have been designed to stop people ever trying to export to Canada. 'And how long before I get paid?' I asked him. 'Oh don't worry,' he said. 'What could be safer than being owed money by the Canadian Government?'

The faxed order finally arrived. I could hardly believe what I was seeing. This guy, who'd talked about vast shipments of beer and had me lashing out on 30,000 new labels – Darleys' minimum order at that time – wanted a paltry fifty cases of Minster Ale. Six hundred bottles. I called him in Canada. 'What the hell is this?' I shouted down the phone. 'Do you realise the hoops I've had to jump through to get this sorted, and the cost of re-labelling? What am I going to with 29,400 leftover labels?'

'Relax,' he said. 'It's just the first step. These are samples. Once I get them to my customers you watch the orders roll in.' We never got a sniff of a follow-up order, and to make things worse we spent six months trying to get his Government to cough up – which they only did after our factors got on the case.

14.
TODAY YORK,
TOMORROW THE WORLD

I soon put the Frank business behind me – but not the 700 cases of Minster Ale we'd produced on the back of his grandiose promises. But that's where God stepped in. I have to assume it was God, because such strokes of good fortune don't usually come my way, and I clearly remember Smithy saying that the only option was to start saying our prayers.

Over the previous few weeks I'd received a couple of letters, maybe more, inviting me to the Singapore World Beer Festival. I dropped them straight in the bin. I was working ridiculously long hours, had an ongoing cash-flow problem and was still fuming over the Canadian saga. What did I want with a trip to the Far East? But the organisers wouldn't give up on me. They started sending faxes, asking me whether I'd received their letters and insisting that they really wanted York Brewery to be represented at their Festival.

Okay, I thought, let's not be rude. They're only trying to do their job. So I replied, and I put it on the line. I told them we were a very young company, that we were fighting tooth and nail to stay afloat, that I was up to my neck in everything from chasing orders to washing out manky casks, and had neither the time nor the money to swan off to Singapore. Next day I got a phone call from a charming gentleman who introduced himself as an ambassador representing the Beer Festival. I can't remember his name, but I'll call him Mister Lee. He told me he would shortly be flying to England where he planned to visit all the breweries that the organisers wished to invite to the Festival. Would I have time to meet with him? It seemed to me that if he was prepared to go to all that trouble, the least I could do was to accommodate him. 'Sure,' I said, 'come on up to York.'

This had started out being mildly irritating. It had seemed utterly irrelevant. How wrong can you be? The man who'd phoned me showed up a few days later – all very smart in his suit and tie and speaking perfect English. I showed him around the brewery, after which we sat in the bar and I spelled out why I could afford neither the time nor the money to visit his homeland. He held up his hand, apologised for interrupting me and asked, 'Please, will you just hear what I have to say before you make a final decision?' I couldn't imagine what he had in mind, but there was no way I was going to refuse to hear him out. He was a model of grace and courtesy – quite a contrast to my pal Frank. He proceeded to explain that the people he represented really did require – not request, but require – my presence at the Festival, jointly funded by the Singapore Government through the Tourist Board, together with a range of business partners. He still wasn't persuading me – but he soon would.

'We appreciate your circumstances, but we have funds in place, and here is what we propose. We can pay for you and an associate to fly out to Singapore. We can accommodate you in a four-star hotel just a stone's throw from the harbour area, which is where the Festival will take place. You will arrive two days before it starts so that you have time to decorate your stand. After the Festival is over we will allow you two days to pack up and wind down before we fly you home again. Would that suit you?' He had my full attention now, but before I could answer he went on, 'Can you tell me how many of your brews you could bring to the Festival? We will require at least two.' I swallowed hard. 'No problem,' I said. 'How about Yorkshire Terrier and, uh, Minster Ale.' Minster Ale! Thanks, Frank, my Canadian chum! 'Good,' he said. 'That will be fine.' 'So,' I asked, anxious to move the conversation on before he started asking probing questions about the difference between the two beers, 'the only cost to us is shipping the beer out to you, is that right?' 'Yes,' he said, 'but you should get that back from what you sell at the Festival; and you can charge a premium price, so you ought to make a handsome profit.'

I hadn't a clue at this stage how many we should plan to ship, but he was already on the case. He pulled out a sheaf of papers and showed me their forecast of numbers attending – locals and tourists. We decided that four pallets ought to be about right. I told him it would be impossible to forecast how many we'd sell and that I couldn't afford to ship any leftovers home – but on the other hand I was unwilling to leave them behind. He even had an answer for that. He was sure he could make a deal with a local bar owner who had a few outlets in the city centre. Of course, I was worried that this might all be pie in the sky, but he was at pains to assure me that in his country a deal was considered sealed once you shook hands, and that to renege on an agreement would be to lose face – something nobody wanted. Nevertheless, he recognised my concerns and agreed to sign a contract.

Smithy agreed to my being absent for ten days, but couldn't resist telling all and sundry that I was 'swanning off on a jolly'. I pointed out that trading hours at the festival were from midday to midnight, six days running. That didn't cut any ice. We were working just as hard at the brewery – and the weather wasn't half as good.

The question now was, who would I take with me? There was no way Smithy was going to let me have anybody from the brewery. We were over-stretched as it was, and work would surely be piling up for me when I got back. 'I know,' I said, 'I'll ask Julie,'

Never miss an opportunity to get in the newspapers...

So there we were, Julie and I, off to Singapore to sell beer. We worked hard, but had a great time – and a couple of ridiculous coincidences. The very first person who came up to us after we'd set up the stall was a fellow wearing one of our Yorkshire Terrier T-shirts. He came from Leeds, and had visited us just a few weeks earlier. We'd no sooner wished this fellow good luck and sent him on his way with a complimentary beer than another Yorkshireman showed up – and not just any Yorkshireman. I recognised him straight away. He was a York taxi driver who had recently delivered a cask of ale for us when his local ran out of beer and we had nobody around to make the run.

There was no let-up in the flow of visitors to the Festival, but as soon as we closed for the day, around midnight, we were free to sample the amazing dishes available in Singapore's huge food market; and we made new friends, including the head brewer and sales manager from the Carlow brewery in Ireland. One night we went to the renowned Madam Wong's Night-Club. It was mobbed, but we found a table and made ourselves comfortable. At three o'clock, time was called. We didn't think much about it, and sat there sipping our drinks. Ten minutes later we were the only people in the entire place and the staff were starting to look edgy. It was a far cry from the Nottingham Playhouse scene, and it was made quite plain that we needed to get out – now. It's simply what you do in Singapore. You obey the rules. The experience gave me an idea that I would later put to good use when we opened our first pub.

My fears about having two beers that were indistinguishable from each other were allayed as soon as we greeted the first visitors to our stall. I'd composed a new set of tasting notes, and I'd chosen my words very carefully indeed. I went no further than claiming that Minster Ale was 'more fruity' than Terrier, with 'a crisper taste' which left more of a 'malty aftertaste on the palate'. I then had the pleasure of watching all these aficionados sniffing their beer, holding it up to the light, tasting it, closing their eyes and nodding agreement with all the claims I'd made for them. Then I heaved a huge sigh of relief.

We sold three of the four pallets of beer we'd shipped out, but I was worried that the bar-owner who'd promised to mop up what was left might not deliver. I tracked down Mister Lee and we went round to his lock-up, where we counted the cases that remained to be sold. Then we set off to find this mystery customer. Our man Mister Lee, in his immaculate suit, pressed shirt and tie, led me down a dingy side-street and into what you'd describe as a proper Chinese-style drinking-den. The bar-tender summoned a muscle-bound guy in dark glasses, who led us through a bead curtain. There we were introduced to the biggest Chinese man I've ever seen. He must have been six foot six, and was built like a heavyweight boxer. He wore jeans and a tight-fitting white T-shirt. His hair came down to his shoulders. His ears were studded with diamonds, and tattoos covered every visible part of his body. He looked like the kind of guy who only ever heard the words 'Yes, boss' wherever he went.

Mister Lee introduced me. I tried not to wince too obviously as my knuckles cracked under the grip of his massive hand. We sat down. One of his minions put a beer in front of me and Mister Lee laid the contract for the beer, plus his inventory for unsold stock, in front of our host. They exchanged a few words, after which Mister Big snapped his fingers. Someone dialled a number on a phone and handed it to him. He spoke for several minutes while we drank our beers and waited. After he put the phone down Mister Lee gathered his papers into his briefcase and stood up. I followed suit, at which point Mister Big crushed my hand again and we were escorted from the premises. As we emerged blinking into the street I asked, 'So when will he pay us?'

Mister Lee grinned at me. 'He already has. That phone call was him wiring the money to your York account. I believe I told you that in Singapore a businessman will never do anything that risks him losing face.'

The major highlight of our stay in Singapore came when I attended a luncheon at which I was due to speak. That's all they told me, that it was a 'luncheon'. I'd envisaged a couple of dozen people sat around some restaurant and me delivering the fifteen-minute talk they were asking for. Even so, I'd spent most of the flight out writing and re-writing my speech and trying to reduce it to a few notes which would prompt me. When we arrived at the venue we found it was in a huge ballroom at a five-star hotel, and a sea of people seated at tables for ten. We ate a superb seven-course meal with plenty of wine. Nerves? Not after that lot.

I'd noticed right away that the seat beside me was

empty, and remained so throughout the meal. They were serving coffee and the speeches had begun when a very elegantly dressed fellow came in and took the vacant seat. He apologised for being late, told me his flight had been delayed, and that he was down to speak before me. However, he added, he needed to organise his slides, and his notes – which, I saw, were typed on fancy Saatchi and Saatchi stationery – and suggested I go first.

My address went well enough, but once my new neighbour got to his feet I offered up a silent prayer of thanks that I didn't have to follow him. It was a superb speech, illustrated with brilliant slides and a wonderful selling pitch as to why his lager ought to be imported into Singapore in quantity. The brand was Cobra, and the speaker was the company's founder, Karan Bilimora, later Lord Bilimora. His beer of course is sold worldwide, although it's brewed not in his native India but in England, by Charles Wells of Bedford.

The Singapore trip had been a surprise, and a very pleasant one. I was learning that in this business you never knew what was around the corner.

It was some time in August when I answered the phone and found that York Minster, or rather the Chapter Clerk, one Brigadier Peter Lyddon, wanted to talk to me. He wasn't happy that we were using the word Minster as a brand label on our bottled beer, and was considering legal action. 'Hold on,' I said, reaching for the Business Directory and flipping it open. 'How about… let's see. Minster Alarms, Minster Auto Alarms, Minster Coachworks, Minster Fish Bar, Minster FM Radio, Minster Hotel, Minster Inn, Minster Law, Minster Skips…? Do you want me to go on?' The Brigadier agreed that there was no actual Minster trade mark but told me it was rather poor form not to have asked his permission before using it. 'Fair enough,' I said. 'I'm sorry.'

As soon as the conversation was over I called *The Press*, who were grateful for such a story on what was, they told me, a pretty slow news day. A few minutes later I got a call from Dan Rutstein, their beer writer, asking me to meet him outside the Minster at midday with a bottle of the contentious product.

I did actually sit down later and write a letter to the Archbishop, David Hope, assuring him that only a beer of exceptional quality and the most delicate taste would be named after such a magnificent structure as York Minster. I also took the opportunity to remind him of all the wonderful beers that were brewed by monks throughout Yorkshire in years gone by. I even suggested that York might take a leaf out of Ripon's book and sell a beer named after their cathedral in their own retail outlet. He did send a reply, and very friendly it was – but I never saw any beer in the cathedral shop. I later learned that the General Synod of the Church of England had discussed the trade-marking of cathedral names shortly before my run-in with the Minster people, but had decided it was not practicable.

While this was all good fun – or seems so in retrospect – we were soldiering on with the business of finding more outlets. Shaz was shoe-horning additional pubs into our rounds, so much so that we were now hiring a second van several days a week; and Keith, our reserve drayman, was now working full-time. On the wholesale side, Wetherspoons and Beer Seller were increasing their orders. Finding a local publican who was willing to try our product, however, remained a huge challenge. When we approached the Black Swan on Peasholme Green, one of York's oldest and most popular pubs, the landlady told us, yes, she would be happy to replace her current guest ale with Yorkshire Terrier. There was only one problem. The ale in question was Timothy

Taylor's Landlord, and a bunch of her regular drinkers told her that if she dared remove their favourite they would seek refreshment elsewhere.

I had a think, then went to see her. 'How about if I invite all these disgruntled regulars to the brewery?' I said. 'Let them see the place, taste the beer – and if they still want to stay with Landlord, fair enough.'

They showed up a couple of weeks later, about twenty of them. I gave them the full, unedited brewery tour, with all the technical and anecdotal material I could muster, then took them to the bar where they got stuck into the Terrier. The next day the landlady from the Black Swan rang to tell me we were on. The lads were happy – if a little hung over – and how soon could I get an eighteen over to her? Over the next few years we sold her several a week. A little while later, we were thrilled when Mike Dandy at the Spread Eagle in Walmgate not only ordered Terrier and Stonewall but also decorated the sign outside the pub with the Brewery logo. Every such advance gave us a boost, and helped raise our profile. Slowly, it seemed, we were making headway in the city – but boy, was it hard work.

As well as making inroads into the York pubs, we were making progress with the bottled beers – although that was a real swings and roundabouts job. We were wildly excited when we were listed with Tesco, less so when we read the small print. The up side was that we would get into thirty of their stores, the down side was that we had to make the deliveries. Some of the stores placed orders for no more than a couple of cases - hardly worth the expense; but, we figured, it was a foot in the door.

We got a foot in the Safeway door too – and promptly got our toes trapped. They ordered three pallets and asked for delivery to their warehouse – much better for us than going to individual stores. No sooner had we dropped them off, however, than the beer buyer was on the phone. 'Congratulations,' he said. 'You've been selected to go on promotion.' 'Oh, great,' I replied. 'Yes, isn't it?' he said. 'It's a buy four and get one free deal. It means that for every fourth beer a customer buys, we'll send you an invoice for a fifth.' 'Hang on,' I said, 'I don't think we can go with that – but thanks anyway.' 'It's not a choice,' he said. 'Well, let me go and crunch some numbers,' I said. 'Then I'll get back to you.'

It didn't take me long to confirm what my guts were telling me. This was a total rip-off. I got back on the phone. 'We'll lose money on this,' I said. 'I'm not sure we can go ahead.' He didn't waste time with niceties. 'Okay,' he said, 'come and collect your beer.' I explained that we were a new, small business working our nuts off to produce a quality product and couldn't survive if we took a beating like he was wanting to dish out. He wouldn't budge. Next day we collected the three pallets and crossed Safeway off our list.

Waitrose had a different approach. They told me that Yorkshire Terrier wouldn't sell around the country. 'Why not?' I asked. 'Too localised,' they said. 'Oh,' I replied. 'You mean like Newcastle Brown?'

We persevered, trying Asda next. They were an obvious choice, being a Yorkshire firm with headquarters in Leeds. And they expressed great enthusiasm for our beer. They started stocking Yorkshire Terrier and it sold well. Then they made a strange request – more of a diktat, to be honest. The big boys don't generally ask you favours; they explain in simple language precisely what you are going to do. In Asda's case it was that the bottles should come in packs of eight rather than twelve. Of course we – and the environment – had to bear the increased costs of packaging.

Overall, then, we were going forward. We even found our cash flow situation easing to the point where we were able to cancel the factoring service at the bank and save a few thousand a year. This gave Roy a new job, which he rather enjoyed. Every time I walked in his office there was a stack of small claims court applications on his desk. Roy would always phone defaulters, then follow up with a couple of letters threatening court action. Then, at the end of the month, if they hadn't paid, there was no messing. He instituted proceedings for monies due, plus costs and interest. In nine cases out of ten the landlords coughed up immediately.

We were doing well with our first two beers and decided it might be time to do another one. Of course, we'd had one-offs like Final Whistle for the football fans, but we were thinking of adding a third to our 'year-round' range. Andrew was keen to brew a strong mild, something based on a seasonal beer we'd produced for the Millennium celebrations. He had in mind a more complex recipe, using torrefied wheat, chocolate malt, roasted barley and crystal malt – and a variety of hops including Bramling Cross, Fuggles and Challenger. At 5.4 per cent ABV it would pack a lot more punch than Stonewall (3.8 per cent) and Terrier (4.2 per cent).

We gave Andrew the go-ahead and waited to see what he produced. When the day came and it was ready to taste we gathered in the bar, all the staff plus a few Brewery Club members. It was a perk we offered them, to partake of a tasting session whenever we had a new brew. So there we were, tongues hanging out, and here it was, coming out of the tap, Andrew and Nick's new sensation – our third permanent brew.

There was a fair amount of slurping, some sighing, and a few murmurs of appreciation. Looking around at everybody's faces, I knew right away we were onto a winner here. It had wonderful flavours, genuine strength, and was a delight to drink. It slid down your throat like dark silk.

We needed a name for the new brew, and I knew exactly what I wanted to call it. Some time previously I'd taken my youngest daughter, Alice, to the York Dungeon. I'd been very impressed by a story they told there – and the picture they used to advertise it. It was about a fellow called Harry Martindale, who was working on a dig under the Treasurer's House. They were uncovering a stretch of Roman road in the cellar. He was all alone when he heard music. He backed off into a corner and from there witnessed a troop of Roman soldiers emerge from the wall and march past him. At first he could only see them from their knees upwards, but as they progressed onto the bit of road that had been uncovered, he could see the rest of their legs as well. For any doubters, Martindale was able to describe in detail their clothing, even down to the manner in which their sandals were laced – details he was unlikely to have known previously. Bearing in mind my run-in with the man from the Minster, I approached the Dungeon. Yes, I could use the artwork from their ad, so long as I mentioned them on the label.

I don't know how many pints of Centurion's Ghost Ale I sank that night at the brewery but by the time my taxi arrived I wasn't the only one who was barely able to walk. Or speak. We had a hit on our hands, and we knew it.

With the earlier success of Final Whistle in mind, we decided to try a few more one-offs. They were a big help to us, being very popular with those pubs that wanted to rack up a score-sheet of different beers and appeal to all those 'anorak' types who tick every new one off their check-list. We knew these places as 'ticker pubs'. We deliberately went for eye-catching or provocative names, anything that might get us a bit of press coverage. When England were playing

Scotland at football, for example, our 'Goodbye Jock' got us noticed by the national press: a paragraph in the *Sun*, no less. Careful not to offend our neighbours north of the border, I was quoted as promising that, in the event of a Scottish victory, I would re-name it 'Goodbye Jack'.

In terms of publicity value, however, there was never a beer to beat 'Bud Bitter'. You don't often hear of real ale fans walking into a pub and asking for a pint of Bud. Perish the thought. But our Bud was different. I can put my hand on my heart and assure you that the name was supposed to conjure up images of springtime: the trees in bud, the daffodils on the city walls about to burst forth. Obvious, really. And when I was asked about the pump-clips, which featured frogs - uncannily like the ones that appeared on Budweiser's TV adverts – I expressed amazement at the coincidence.

Bud Bitter hadn't been in the pubs many days when I heard from London-based lawyers representing Anheuser-Busch, the people behind the American Budweiser, threatening me with legal action. Think sledgehammers and nuts. They were quite clear about what they wanted me to do – namely, withdraw the product from the market and destroy all advertising and promotional material. Did I have a choice? Yes, of course I did: do as they said or see them in court.

I decided to meet them halfway. We changed the name to Bug Bitter, removed the frog and replaced it with a crocodile. Then I faxed a copy of the new artwork to the lawyers. They weren't amused – or pretended they weren't. I could have sworn, when they rang me, that they were grinning from ear to ear. They told me that their clients had used crocs in an advertising campaign a couple of years previously, so would I stop taking the piss?

I decided to go along with them. Why make enemies? I changed the croc to a praying mantis – a species of bug, geddit? – and faxed that off. They still weren't happy, and were back on the phone explaining why. 'Our clients consider that "Bug" is too much like "Bud",' they told me.

'Now it's them taking the piss,' I said. 'Tell them I'll see them in court.' I almost fancied going to litigation and exposing their bullying tactics to the press, but I was denied the opportunity. They never called back.

The outcome of all this was good local and national press coverage, and the icing on the cake was when *Look North*, the BBC's regional news programme, sent a crew out to do a feature on us. The cameraman and the presenter were easily seduced into the bar after shooting, and both signed up as members, regularly bringing a gang of mates in on a Friday night. For the feature, I was asked to comment on Anheuser-Busch's UK regional director, who was quoted as saying, 'We have a duty to our customers to make sure that when they order a Bud they're given our beer.' Not in our visitor centre, they didn't. Before this all blew up we'd already started selling the real Budweiser, the one from Czechoslovakia – who had had their own run-ins with Anheuser-Busch over the years. It was a much superior product, so I was happy to reply, 'If a customer asks for a Bud in York Brewery they get the real thing – all the way from the Czech Republic.'

All these beers I've mentioned were, of course, one-offs. Nothing wrong with them, but they had a limited appeal and a short life-span. On the plus side, they gave our brewers a chance to try different recipes and this gave them the opportunity to come up with something special. We were determined to add a fourth beer to our regulars. I threw out the challenge to Andrew and Nick: a fruity, pale bitter with an ABV of 3.6 per cent, a good reliable session beer. The lads surpassed themselves, producing another classic brew. We all, loved it straight away and were convinced we were onto a winner.

All we needed was a name, and everyone was looking at me. I held my hands up: I'd set the bar pretty high with Centurion's Ghost and they couldn't expect me to top that. But nobody else had any idea either. Then one morning I was walking past Roy's office. I stuck my head in and said, 'Hey, Roy. We need a name for this new bitter.' I was about to ask him if he'd any suggestions, but he didn't even let me get the words out. He looked up from his keyboard, blinked at me and said, 'Guzzler,' and resumed the task in hand. If only it was always that easy. Guzzler was destined for a series of medals, including a gold at the Society of Independent Brewers (North) awards in 2006 and 2007 – and at the time of writing accounts for 70 per cent of the brewery's output.

Every time I was interviewed for a newspaper piece I was asked the same questions, the ones that well-wishers and even competitors asked me, over and over. How are your sales? Who are your customers?

And every time I found myself trotting out my favourite fact, that we were doing better in Essex than in our own fair city. It was getting beyond a joke – especially as, when a pub did take us on, they very soon sold out. For some time we had been in some of York's better known boozers – the Maltings, the Black Swan, and the Spread Eagle.

Now Shaz had got a toehold in a whole string of pubs: the Bay Horse in Marygate, the First Hussar (North Street), the Golden Ball in Bishophill, the Lendal Cellars, the Punch Bowl and the Swan down Bishopthorpe Road. She now had the ever-helpful Ron Hawkins at the Charles XII in Heslington, and his son Jason at the Keystones in Goodramgate, on the roster. But despite these successes, I was bitterly disappointed not to have more support for a local beer that was winning awards at CAMRA festivals around the country.

The last straw, for me, came when we heard from the Business Development Manager of a certain pub chain that they were ditching Terrier. 'But why?' I asked. 'It's selling as fast as we can supply it.' 'Precisely,' he said. 'It's adversely affecting the sales of other beers.' 'What beers are you talking about?' I asked. That's when he delivered the killer line. 'Beers that rake in a higher profit,' he said. I tried to explain that he was getting more customers in his pub, not all of them Terrier drinkers – meaning that other beer sales went up too. But his mind was made up, and we were out.

There were other blows, reminders that in this business you really were prey to the whims of the marketplace. One minute you're all the rage, the next minute you're out in the wilderness. Around this time, the late 1990s, there was a company called Century Inns who owned all the Tap and Spile pubs. They contacted us to say that we had been voted by their customers as being in their top ten favourite brewers over the past year. A month later we had a short, snappy letter from the same company to say that they had been bought up, and guess what? The new owners would not be taking our beers. I just had time to calculate that that was five to ten barrels a week down the Swanee River – and file the letter in the waste-bin - when Andrew popped into the office to tell me that the owner of Dent Brewery had called in to pick up some beer on behalf of a wholesaler. Could I break off for a natter, as a matter of courtesy? The fact was, I wasn't feeling too sociable. I was livid about this Tap and Spile business and was not in the mood to talk to anyone. 'No,' I said, 'tell him I'm busy.'

I can't really remember why that stuck in my mind, but

at the next SIBA (Society of Independent Brewers) meeting I did notice a particular guy who never spoke, just shot me a dirty look every so often. It was in fact several years later that I figured it all out. We were at a conference together. During a break we were both helping ourselves to the buffet – he at one end of the table and I at the other. As we worked our way towards the middle he could contain himself no longer. 'Hey you,' he shouted. I looked up, as did half the assembled company. 'Yes, you from York. I picked up a load of beer from you, and not so much as a coffee, not even a hello, you just sat there in your bloody office lording it.'

I'd clearly committed a major faux pas, and had no idea how badly he'd taken it - nor how long he would nurse his resentment. So if he's reading this, I can only say how sorry I am and hope he forgives me.

My dissatisfaction with our beer sales in York continued to vex me. It was time for me and Smithy to repair to that hotbed of inspiration, the Deramore Arms, and generate the next big idea. I got the first round and kicked things off. 'Okay,' I said, 'my view is we need to get seriously involved in the marketplace.' 'Right,' he said. 'Tell me sommat I don't already know.' 'Okay, how about we open our own pub, slap bang in the city centre. Let the buggers know we mean business.' Smithy grinned as he raised his glass to mine. 'Hey, I'll drink to that,' he said. 'No bloody problem. Only one thing.' 'Go on,' I said. 'How do we pay for it?' 'Ah. I'm working on that. But in principle..?' 'In principle, absolutely bleeding spot on. Let's go for it.'

That was the easy part, deciding to give it a go. The reasons stacked up convincingly: it would raise our profile, really announce us as a presence in York, and give us another profit centre. But money and availability of suitable premises were sticking points because the moment anything worth looking at came on the market it was always going to be snapped up by the voracious pub chains – or a national or regional brewer with the cash and clout to outbid us.

We soon came to the obvious conclusion, that the only way to get our own pub was to find an empty building and obtain a drinks licence – plus planning permission for change of use. As to the money required for re-modelling and paying for a lease, I reckoned there was every chance that one of the large brewers might, in return for us stocking their beers, cough up some money as a loan or investment.

I approached several of the majors and before long attracted interest from Bass. They were in fact by far the keenest, and promised that once we'd found a place they would survey it and let us know what kind of deal they could offer. I soon found a premises on King's Square, handily placed within spitting distance of the Shambles. Previously an estate agent's office, it was now owned by Langley's the solicitors. I made enquiries and learned that Langley's were open to offers, also willing to consider a change of use. The police had no objections, which just left the planning committee. It was pretty much as before. I had two minutes to put my case, which I tried to sum up in a few forceful points. We could not get a foothold in York. Almost all the pubs were owned by chains or big brewers, most of whom wouldn't entertain a small local brewery. If they did, they expected massive discounts – and would drop us on a whim; or get taken over and leave us to sink or swim. We had even lost accounts because we sold too much beer. The only way to secure a reliable local market for our product was to have our own pub. We were currently selling six different beers in the Brewery Club, but only two of them could be savoured around town. We currently sold more beer in Essex… at this point I felt like a loop of tape playing the same old song over and over. I added that the pub would provide a number of new full-time and part-time posts as well as securing jobs in the brewery. I reassured them that the atmosphere and décor would be traditional, wholesome, discerning – with quality products served in clean, safe surroundings.

There were a couple of written objections regarding noise, but the vote in our favour was unanimous. All we needed now was for Bass to stump up the readies and we were on our way. However, despite several meetings with them, nothing was getting firmed up. Langleys were huffing and puffing at the delay. I had negotiated a 'stepping-stone' rent which went up every year for the first five then in five-year stages to the end of the twenty-five year period we had in mind. It was all very reasonable. Even Smithy was relaxed about it – especially since Bass were going to put £90,000 into the project. Weren't they?

We got as far as a meeting at which Bass were to cross the T's and dot the I's on the agreement. And that's when they pulled out. They calmly stated that they had lost confidence in the arrangement and preferred to invest their shareholders' money elsewhere. I was shell-shocked. To compound our misery, two days later I got a letter from Langleys saying they were fed up waiting, and would put the building back on the market if we didn't sign the lease by the following Friday. On the plus side, we had here a building bang in the middle of town in a prime location with massive footfall – a liquor licence in place and planning approved. We couldn't just give up now. The down side was… no money.

Monday morning I got a call from Sally at our solicitors' office. She sounded all bright and breezy. 'Hi Tony, great news.' I waited. 'I've got the lease ready for you. Just needs you to pop down the office and sign it.' I agreed that we'd be down the next day, around three o'clock. I decided against breaking the news about Bass. I just called Smithy and alerted him to the situation. Next afternoon we showed up as requested. I explained to Sally what had happened. She was genuinely sorry to hear it and immediately started putting away the papers she had laid out on her desk. 'So that's that then,' she said. 'No,' I said. 'It isn't.'

'You can't possibly sign a twenty-five-year lease without any money behind you,' she protested. But she knew I wasn't going to budge. She turned to Smithy, the sensible one. 'Tony,' she said, 'you can't sign. It would be crazy. Tell him.' He didn't say anything, just looked at me. 'Look,' she said, 'I can't force you, but it would be going against my professional principles if I didn't do everything in my power to stop you.' Smithy looked at Sally, then at me. 'If he's signing, so am I,' he said.

I still see Sally from time to time and she still can't get over the fact that (a) we signed it, and (b) that she was powerless to stop us, despite hitting us with all her professional rhetoric.

After the signing Smithy and I went to the place where I'd licked so many wounds in the past, from my many batting failures for Heslington CC, to the day I was sacked by Little Chef, to the many crises that had buffeted us as we built up the business – the Deramore Arms, home to our many, many brainstorming sessions. The subject before us this time was, were we being incredibly brave or utterly stupid? And, as leaseholders on a city centre property, where in the name of all we held sacred were we going to find £100,000 for building works?

15.
HAPPY CHRISTMAS –
THE SELECTION BOXES ARE ON ME

I still had a personal life – and that wasn't going so great either. I was still without a car, and a licence, and I wasn't at all happy with my rabbit-hutch of a flat at Heworth. It was a ten-minute walk to the local shop if I wanted so much as a pint of milk and a packet of fags; and the couple who lived upstairs were still keeping me awake at night – or rather their squeaky bed-springs were. I needed to buy my own place.

I looked around and spotted a two-up two-down terraced house on Hull Road, right next-door to an off-licence on one side and Kwiksave on the other. Perfect. The owner was asking £44,000, but I was pretty confident I could knock him down. He'd rented it out to DHSS tenants for three years and it wasn't exactly gleaming inside. The kitchen looked like a back-street kebab shop on a Sunday morning. I pitched in with an offer, which was rejected at first, but it wasn't long before the agent came back to me and asked whether I'd take it at £40,000. I managed to arrange a mortgage – those were the days! – and sealed the deal. When Christmas came that year, 1999, I remember sitting down and reflecting that we were almost four years into the project and still paying ourselves an annual salary of £10,000.

The business was picking up nicely, but every penny we earned was being ploughed back in. So there I was, still skint, so much so that all my kids got from Santa Claus was a selection box of chocolates each. I even had to cadge a lift in Phil's car to get down to the Midlands, and get my Dad to pick me up at Woodhall Services on the M1. However, I was now a home-owner once more, so things must be looking up. The location suited me down to the ground, and, just around the corner, lived Alice – who was still a good friend and willing listener to my tales of woe. We spent a lot of evenings putting the world to rights. She was looking for Mister Right and I was lamenting the state of the brewing industry.

Around this time I got a letter from middle daughter Emma, who'd started school at Rugby, where her mother was a teacher. She was very unhappy and wanted to tell me all about it. It was heart-rending. She wanted to leave, right away. She would live with me and go to York College. I took another look at my new abode, ripped out all the carpets, then went into Kwiksave where I filled a trolley with the most powerful de-greaser I could find, plus several large tins of magnolia paint. A few weeks later I'd transformed the house.

It wasn't perfect, but it was clean and had that delicious smell of fresh paint. Alice was pretty handy working with wood, and after a bit of haggling over a suitable hourly rate laid a pine floor in the living-room. A real touch of class. Between her frequent trips to the States, Julie was also providing that indefinable woman's touch around the place.

By the time I'd got all my furniture out of storage – and Phil's garage – I reckoned I had a halfway decent place that my daughter would enjoy sharing. I remained hectically busy at the brewery; Emma had her time full with college and all the other things that sixteen-year-olds get up to, and we settled into a really warm and delightful relationship, a time that we will always treasure – so long as we gloss over the trauma of my trying to teach her to drive. As for Emma's college career, that's a story I saved for many years, and took out of cold storage when she married Jason, her kite-surfing instructor, in 2015. As a dutiful father attending her first parents' evening, I was little concerned when two of the teachers I spoke to mentioned her patchy attendance record. After introducing myself to a third, I decided to take the lead. I opened with, 'Emma's got a great personality, hasn't she?' The teacher thought for a moment, then replied, 'I'm sure she has, and I'm very much looking forward to meeting her.'

With my domestic life looking a little more settled, I turned my attention to the search for cash, and lots of it. The one bright spot was that I had done a deal with Langleys whereby our first three months in the premises on King's Square would be rent-free. I'd argued for this on the basis that we would spend the time on building works and would inevitably find unexpected expenses arising. I'd had plans drawn up by Guy Moorey, a local architect who had been recommended to me. He in turn had introduced me to a builder, Adrian Taylor. The word was that, although he was a small operator, he had worked on a few pubs in York and was capable of thinking outside the box.

Meanwhile I was phoning round all the breweries and pub companies who might be interested in an investment, and getting nowhere – unless you count the odd one or two who promised to talk it over and get back to me.

We'd had an unexpected snag over the acquisition of a

liquor licence – but it had a good outcome. Langleys, who owned the freehold, insisted I hire the services of a specialist consultant in licensing, a firm called Poppleton Allen from Nottingham. I couldn't see the need for this, at all, and was confident that I could handle the business, as I had done with the Brewery Club. I would use Mark Hepworth at Denison Till, whose charges would be very reasonable.

However, Langleys made it plain that I had no choice. They gave me a phone number and told me to ask for a fellow named Jeremy Allen, one of the founding partners. He did the things he was required to do and when we got a date for the hearing he came up to York. I showed him round the brewery and we went for a meal at the very up-market Blue Bicycle in Walmgate. At this stage I still thought we were getting into bed with Bass. On the brewery tour I'd told Jeremy about our cash-flow issues and he agreed to pay for the meal if I bought the wine. That put me at my ease. This was a guy I could get on with.

The meal lived up to its billing and the wine was superb. We were on the brandies and coffee. Time to raise the delicate question. I braced myself and asked, 'And what sort of figure are we looking at – for your services?'

It tripped off his tongue as if it was the most natural thing in the world. 'Oh, about a grand.' I'd like to think I did a bit of canny negotiating that night, but I suspect Jeremy took pity on me. Either way, by the time we'd sunk our final brandy he had agreed to waive the fee and bring his staff up to York for a tour of the brewery – with their partners. As much beer as they could drink, plus snacks, as payment for his services. In the end it suited both sides – although the bill for the wine made my eyes water.

Having bonded with Jeremy, I decided to call him a few days later and explain the difficulty we were in with Bass.

Did he know anybody who fancied a pub partnership – someone, that is, who would stump up all the initial set-up costs? He promised to have a think and get back to me. I remember putting the phone down and thinking, yeah, yeah, yeah – it's what they all say.

To my surprise he got back to me the very next day. He told me he'd put me in touch with a guy called Chris Holmes, M.D. of a company called Tynemill who had a few pubs in the Nottingham-Derby area. He said, 'He's expecting your call,' and with that he gave me the guy's number and wished me luck. When I called Chris, he answered straight away. After a short conversation, in which I outlined our situation and aims, he said, 'Okay, I'll hop on a train tomorrow morning.' Suddenly, things were happening – fast.

He showed up around eleven and came directly to the brewery. I took to Chris right away. He had no airs and graces, and displayed an impressive knowledge of the brewing industry – as he should have done, being a former Chairman of CAMRA. In addition, in his younger days he'd taught Economics at Nottingham University before taking a huge gamble, buying the old Kings Arms in Newark. The gamble paid off, and within a few years he had a string of twelve pubs to his name. One of them, which was within shouting distance of the Inland Revenue Offices, he re-named The Vat and Fiddle.

Next door was the old Bramcote Brewery which in due course he bought up. At the same time he ditched the name Tynemill and re-branded the company Castle Rock, soon transforming it into a 350-barrels-a-week affair. So Chris was pretty dynamic, and I was excited to have attracted his interest. He told me he was looking to expand. Having seen around our place he was clearly impressed – and he took an immediate liking to our beer. So far, so good. I walked him into town, and up and down Colliergate before opening up the premises on Kings Square and rolling out the plans we'd had drawn up. Chris liked what he saw, and suggested a couple of changes, both of which made sense to me.

We adjourned to one of my favourite pubs, the Blue Bell on Fossgate, one of the oldest and smallest pubs in York, which still had many of its original features. Smithy joined us for a couple of pints, and an hour later we were shaking hands on a deal. We would set up a new company named after a one-off beer we'd recently brewed. The Mildly Mad Pub Co. Ltd seemed to suit our mood and situation. The company would be half owned by the York Brewery, half by Castle Rock. The new pub would be added to Chris' stable, and he would take on all the admin matters while we appointed a manager and staff and undertook the day to day running. As for the money, Castle Rock would supply all required funds as a straightforward loan. I would crack on with organising the building work immediately, while Chris got the finance in place.

We were all delighted with the deal. After seeing Chris off on the train Smithy and I went and celebrated with a couple more beers. This was a red-letter day. We'd found a partner to fund us, a guy with a great track record, a brilliant career in our industry and, to add icing to the cake, a guy we both liked. In all our many dealings with Chris over the years I can only once recall him mentioning the fact that he'd 'bailed us out'; and I can forgive him for that. We were in the middle of some pretty animated negotiations about the prices the Brewery were charging the pub for the beer. But all our problems were resolved with a handshake and a beer, so all credit to Chris. The perfect business partner.

Adrian Taylor, our builder, started work in May 2000. The biggest problem was the cellar. There was an existing one right underneath the spot where we planned to serve the beer. Very handy, except that it was tiny. We considered using the open area out the back, but really we wanted to exploit the little yard as a place where people could enjoy any fine weather that came our way.

I started shopping around for a cellar design company who could come up with a solution. I drew up a short-list and faxed an estimate of the dimensions of the cellar to be dug out. The first reply was a flat refusal to contemplate such a venture. The second consisted of a drawing of two firkins sitting opposite each other. Without thinking, I replied, 'Are you taking the piss?' Their answer didn't take long. 'You started it,' they said. Fortunately, the third reply was from a lovely man called Ken, owner-operator of Hijack, a Harrogate firm. He had given the problem some thought, and came up with a canny system, a telescopic stillage, with all the casks tethered by ropes attached to a system of pulleys. This would enable one person, working alone, to get hold of an 18-gallon cask, lift it up, draw out the stillage, lower the cask, then push it back into place. It was pure genius, to borrow a phrase from Guinness. With this system, and staff adequately trained, we would be able to operate five hand-pulls at a time.

When it came to finding a manger I already had someone in mind. I was selling a lot of Yorkshire Terrier to the Golden Ball in Bishophill. The landlord there was a guy called Don Butler. His son James had been running the Cock and Bottle in Skeldergate. Hearing that we needed a manager, he came knocking at our door. We liked James straight away. He was a chip off the old block: gregarious, with a sharp sense of humour and a natural, easy-going personality.

The builders were in, and the pub was taking shape, but we still hadn't come up with a name. I had a bit of think and it soon came to me.

Happy Christmas – The Selection Boxes Are On Me

When I was eighteen my mates at catering college bought me a tankard. At the bottom, on the inside, was a picture of highwayman suspended from the gallows, and underneath it the legend 'The Last Drop'. I'd always thought that would be a great name for a pub, especially in York, where the notorious Dick Turpin was hanged on the Knavesmire in 1739 and buried in the cemetery at St George's church, Fishergate. So we christened the place The Last Drop Inn, and I set about scouring the bric-a-brac shops for pictures of highwaymen, pistols, and stories about Dick Turpin and Black Bess. I gave a lot of thought to it. This wasn't a suburban local. It was a city-centre establishment with masses of tourists walking by it, all day every day. I always had a certain style in mind – sort of olde worlde, with a false wooden floor in the main seating area to the front, the area that the public would see as they walked in through the door. In the upper bar area we laid York stone flags.

There was a big shop window facing the street, absolutely not the kind of thing you'd expect in a traditional pub. But I wanted to retain it. With so many pubs, you see people walk in and have a look around before deciding whether it's for them. A bunch of men on a night out, and certainly women, will want to know what kind of clientele is inside, what the atmosphere's like, what beer they're selling, maybe even check out the décor. If you can't see the interior from the street, you're taking a risk. So the window stayed.

Opposite the bar, which had to be pretty small, given the shape and size of what we had, we installed a bench, putting it at such a level that people sitting there were at eye level with those standing at the raised barrels we were using as tables. This was the idea I'd seen, and filed away, when we were at Madam Wong's night-club in Singapore.

On the upper floor was an area comprising five rooms

– and ripe for conversion to overnight accommodation. We toyed with the idea of offering B&B, but there was no space for a fire escape, so we asked James if he fancied living over the shop. He took a look and agreed it was a good idea. We gave him a few hundred pounds and left him to spruce it up. Meanwhile we appointed an assistant manager. Vernon was the son-in-law of Roy, our office organiser, and had done the job in a number of hotels. He seemed an ideal fit.

As the builders moved out, we applied the finishing touches. We had a few York Brewery mirrors made, and scattered a miscellaneous collection of tables and chairs around the place. These came our way through a club member David Hulme who had a business in Tadcaster, putting new furniture into pubs and removing the old – quite a bit of which suited our tastes perfectly.

With competition for the tourists' attention so fierce, I wanted to make sure we had good stand-out signs – ones that wouldn't get damaged by the weather. I knew from experience that when a pole sign, or the lights that lit up the words Little Chef, were out, sales suffered. An old friend, Steve, agreed to install three big down-lighters outside the Last Drop at cost if I threw in a few cases of Terrier. So I got the job done cheap, and won us another loyal customer – namely, his son, who after helping him out became a convert to the delights of cask ale, and a regular visitor to the pub.

16.
'WE CAN'T HAVE PEOPLE
ENJOYING THEMSELVES'

The opening night of the Last Drop Inn was to be an all-ticket affair for local VIPs, our suppliers, contractors – including a bus-load from Nottingham for the Castle Rock team – and, of course, a number of York Brewery club members. There was also a press contingent, and the pub would be officially opened by Chris Titley, beer writer for *The Evening Press* as it was in those days. There was just one problem. The date we'd chosen, Tuesday 1st August 2000, just happened to coincide with Trade Day at the Great British Beer Festival at Olympia.

Smithy and I had always rewarded the full-time staff with a trip down to Olympia for the Trade Day. We always entered at least one of our permanent brews for competition. This year it was Yorkshire Terrier, and we had every reason to celebrate. In the Best Bitter category we came second, in the Champion Beer of Britain section third. It was a fantastic achievement.

Thrilled as I was, I couldn't hang about and enjoy the celebrations. I had to get a train back to York for the grand opening of the pub. Some days your luck is in. Simple as that. I got on the train, got settled in my seat and as we pulled out of Kings Cross ordered a beer from the trolley. Terrier! I'd recently been in negotiations with GNER about selling our beer on the train for a three-month period and here it was. I watched the scenery flash by with a big daft grin on my face.

I reflected on the whole process of setting up a new pub, and on recruiting staff. I recalled the moment when I was approached by a potential employee in the most bizarre circumstances. Heslington were playing at Mille Crux, home of Rowntrees. I believe it got the name – which means a thousand crosses – because of all the plague victims buried there. I remember it was a scorching hot day. When we lost our sixth wicket we still needed around fifty to win. Coming in at number eight was a young lad who bowled decent off-breaks and could bat a bit, a player who was blessed with oodles of natural ability but lacked that positive attitude which makes a good sportsman. I walked up to him and gave him a serious pep talk. I reminded him that this was a critical situation, and if he played to his potential we might just pull off a great victory and achieve heroic status; maybe a free pint or two. He listened to every word, prodding the pitch with his bat and nodding agreement as I pressed home my point. Just as I touched his glove and turned to go back to the crease he said, 'Tony, you got any jobs going at the Last Drop Inn?'

At York station I stopped to buy a *Press*. On an inside page was the story about our success, with Andrew quoted as saying that we were standing by for an influx of new orders. 'This is a great day for us,' he added, 'and it's great to be able to offer an award-winning beer on opening night at our first pub.'

'We Can't Have People Enjoying Themselves.'

They tell me it was a super night at the Last Drop Inn but all I remember is calling my brother next day to thank him and his girl-friend for taking me home and seeing me into bed. I can only assume I had enjoyed myself. That opening night set the tone for a huge success. Sales were way beyond our expectations. As well as the usual pub crowd there was the 'what's all the fuss about' crowd and a lot of locals curious to try the new brew. The food too was going well, but the thing that seemed to get everybody talking was the list of pub rules that Shaz had chalked up in huge block letters: NO KIDS, NO JUKE BOX, NO POOL, NO TAPED MUSIC, NO COIN-IN-SLOT MACHINES, NO DARTS!

The vast majority of people we spoke to liked our approach. It wasn't for everybody; we knew that – but as far as we were concerned Sharon's sign told it like it was: this just wasn't going to be one of those noisy boozers full of flashing lights and loud music. The only background sound we wanted was people talking and laughing, and the occasional clink of glasses. And it worked: we were packed, night after night. Even so, there was often some clever sod trying to tell us what we were doing wrong. One night a woman who ran pleasure-boat trips along the river told me, 'You can't run a business like that – a great long list of what you don't allow.' I put on my most serious face – grim, some people have called it – and told her, 'The fact is, love, we don't want people enjoying themselves.'

Our double whammy, winning medals at the Beer Festival and having such a successful opening night, was a massive boost to morale – and to the business. It got the phones ringing as people called in with orders and enquiries. As if by magic the pub opening seemed to have announced us as a serious business whose management knew what they were doing. It truly was a landmark moment.

P*** Up In A Brewery

With lift-off finally happening, one or two perks started to come our way. Chris Holmes invited me to go to Prague and visit the Staropramen brewery. It was an out-and-out jolly, and nobody made any pretence about it: I was along for the ride, and the beer – and I thoroughly enjoyed both. Neil Kellett, secretary of Castle Rock and Mildly Mad, was with us on the trip. The trip was funded by Coors, a major supplier to Castle Rock's pubs and hosted by Gary Beagley, their business development officer. The only fly in the ointment was getting a call from my daughter to say that some toe-rag had burgled our pied-a-terre down Hull Road. They'd got away with a dodgy telly, a set of knackered golf-clubs, and a crappy old stereo, so there was a fair chance that they might electrocute themselves. I called Emma to see whether she was okay and got Julie to go over and make quite certain.

The tour of Staropramen Brewery was a special experience. The place is huge, with floor after floor of open fermenters – square rather than round, and each holding 120 barrels. Back in York, Chris was so impressed with Shaz's blackboards he got her to show him some other examples of her work around York. It wasn't long before he'd invited her to Nottingham to do some work for the Castle Rock estate. On hearing that, Smithy, who'd spotted the chemistry told me, 'I think we'll be needing a new sales lady before long.' He was dead right. Chris offered her a job as manager of Coopers, a famous old pub in Burton, and she all but snapped his hand off. So it was fond farewells all round, a dinner at the Viceroy and off you go. We were sorry to lose her, but we'd had a potential successor lined up for some time.

I'd long been a fan of Barbara Vincent, who'd been doing great work at the bar and with the tours. I was sure she would be capable of handling landlords, wholesalers, supermarket beer buyers and all the other potentially

awkward people we had to deal with. She would have her hands full, so we found her a full-time assistant, a very smart young lass called Emma Lund.

It was around this time that Smithy tried to defy the laws of physics and fit two firkins of beer in his hatch-back, a clapped-out Fiat 127. It was tea-time, our drayman had finished for the day, and we'd had a call from a customer who'd run short. He was just down the A1 and Smithy volunteered to drop them off on his way back to Leeds. It had been a while since Smithy had handled a firkin in anger. Andrew and I stood at the gallery window and watched as he huffed and puffed and somehow got them into the car. We offered shouts of encouragement, laced with abuse. They call it banter these days. We even clapped as he stood back, heaved a sigh of relief and reached up to close the hatch. And then we laughed. And cried, and fell about. The firkins were bigger than he realised, and went straight through the rear windscreen, showering him with fragments of glass.

My first lesson in marketing, and the one that's stayed

with me, came when I read the words of Henry Ford, the man who brought car ownership to the masses in the USA. When asked why he poured vast sums into marketing he replied, 'Well, I know that fifty per cent of our marketing is effective. Trouble is, nobody can tell me which fifty per cent.'

If you can measure the success of a marketing strategy then you should do it. We made a point, when tourists visited the brewery, of asking them how they got to hear about us. It soon became clear it was through the leaflets we delivered to guest-houses, hotels, pubs and such places.

Now that we were attracting visitors we wanted to sell them stuff. It's called merchandise. We'd enlarged the visitor centre and bar, and had an area designated as the Brewery Shop. So, what would we stock? Or, what would people buy? We already had what we thought were the obvious items, like pens, badges, glasses, tankards, key-rings and so on, but needed a wider range. I was at this time on nodding terms with a guy called Graham Chadwick, a regular at the Deramore Arms in Heslington, and the Charles. One evening I overheard him talking about T-shirts. I walked over and introduced myself. It turned out that Chaddy had his own clothing business in Tadcaster and did a lot of work for breweries and pub chains. It wasn't long before we were stocking a nice range of York Brewery T-shirts and sweat-shirts – and all the staff were sporting a natty polo shirt. That too went on sale – in blue or black, with our logo on the left breast, and 'Yorkshire Terrier' on the right sleeve.

One of the hottest-selling bits of merchandise came our way accidentally when I got chatting to a guy named Jim Somerville. He had his own business, Slaphead Designs, so named because their esteemed owner was as bald as a billiard-ball. He came up with this great idea, namely producing a poster in the style of the London Underground map, but instead of stations having York pubs. He called it the York Overground and did a customised version featuring our logo, and one of our beer labels in each corner. We offered it in a tube or framed and sold a ton, especially at Christmas.

We still hadn't found the best way to sell the bottled beer in the shop. People will readily buy a bottle of wine; not so with beer. A solution arrived when we found a firm that would produce three- and four-bottle cardboard packs, so designed that they would leave the labels visible. When York's annual Food and Drink Festival came around, and the St Nicholas' Fair, we hired a stall on Parliament Street and sold shed-loads in our smart new York Brewery carrier bags.

Once you get into merchandising you start seeing opportunities everywhere you go. Julie and I took a holiday in California, driving up the Pacific coast between Los Angeles and San Francisco. We called in at every microbrewery we came across, and were impressed by the tasting trays they all had which allowed customers to sample as many as six or eight of their brews in one session. As soon as we returned I had a word with Barbara Vincent's husband 'Pop', who was very handy with wood and promised to come up with a design. A call to the Customs and Excise people revealed that we would have to serve our tasters in proper glasses, each stamped with a measured amount of fluid ounces. As soon as we'd found a supplier who could supply me one-third pint glasses and get them stamped, Pop got to work on a design for the trays. He produced ten, each one holding four glasses. They proved very popular.

Having the shop was a bit of an eye-opener. It didn't

Marketing is vital in any business — get your name out at every opportunity...

occur to me at first that we could put almost any brewery-related items in there and people would snap them up. The first example was pump-clips. Every time we did a special brew we had to order a ton of them to get the unit cost down, and that invariably meant that we had more than we could use. So we put them in the shop at 50p a throw. They each had some sort of cartoon figure or motif pertinent to the name, and people seemed to find them irresistible. As for our Christmas specials such as Stocking Filler or Cracker – each of which was adorned with a skimpily clad lovely – they couldn't get enough.

The same thing happened with towels. When we first put them on top of the bar people were nicking them right left and centre, so we put them in the shop at £1.50 a throw. Beer-mats, which had been disappearing since the very first tour group passed through, were another hit at 10p.

We found a surprising new income stream after we were approached by Munton's the maltsters from Stowmarket. They wanted to know whether they could make up a forty-pint home-brew kit for Terrier and Stonewall. The idea was for us to supply the recipe while they did the artwork and packaging and sold it through the speciality beer shops they supplied up and down the country. Nick and Andrew were a bit sceptical at first, but they tried the kits and were very favourably impressed, so we put them on sale, along with four-pint carry-kegs – and 34-pint Pollypins. Throw in glass yards of ale for the dedicated drinker, various pottery items, postcards, bottle-openers, watches, notebooks, pencil-cases, pens, CAMRA publications and our unique Yorkshire Terrier statuettes and you might say we left no stone unturned in our efforts to diversify. We even extended our clothing range to include jackets, ties, baseball caps and shorts. We only ever had one complaint that I can remember, and that was from a club member who said he'd been reprimanded for wearing his Last Drop T-shirt, complete with its picture of a strangled victim, in the works' gym. But then he was a serving officer at H.M. Prison, Full Sutton.

I'd never been a fan of the I.T. culture, but it was obvious that we needed a presence on the internet. Fortunately my brother Robin agreed to build us a website for no fee. All we had to do was provide him with whatever info he required to keep it current. It wasn't an all-singing, all-dancing site, but it got our name and our news out there.

One way and another, we were thriving. The two businesses fed off each other, with the tours helping to spread the word beyond the city walls. And of course we were always looking out for new ways to promote our image. Some of the most successful businesses in the world have found over the years that building up a sort of myth about their history – or a legend – helps form a bond with their customer base. Think Hovis and northern landscapes. Think Marlboro Man. We had always been aware of the links between Centurion's Ghost Ale and York's Roman past, and we now realised that York was promoting its image as Europe's most haunted city. Somewhere I came across a lovely map of the city, showing all the old Roman roads, one of which passed right under the brewery site. I hung it in the bar, and added a few words underneath suggesting that this might explain the regular disappearance in the night of several pints of Ghost. It was a talking point – and we couldn't get enough of those.

Alive to the possibilities, James Butler at the Last Drop decided that they really ought to have their own resident phantom. The problem was, nobody had ever seen or heard anything remotely other-worldly in the place, despite some serious after-hours drinking. So they decided to do some

creative thinking. This was a beautiful old building, smack bang in the middle of York, just a short drunken stagger from the historic Shambles. It needed a show-stopper for the media – and it got one that went all the way – to the *Daily Mirror*, and to an Air America in-flight magazine, to name but two.

The story James and his fellow conspirators came up with went back to 17th century, when the site of the brewery was home to a glazing business owned and run by a Mr Bagshot. He had a lucrative contract, producing replacement glass for the Minster, as well as for local businesses within the city walls. He had high hopes for his beautiful daughter who would, he hoped, marry into the gentry. So when he learned that one of his humble employees, a certain Charles Kimmeridge, had become enamoured with her – and she with him – he determined to put a stop to the romance. The lovers resisted, tensions grew and in the winter of 1652 young Kimmeridge was sacked. Barely a week later Bagshot surprised the pair, on the factory premises, in flagrante. A fight erupted, Bagshot overcame the young man and threw him into the furnace, pushing him into the molten glass with a long metal pole. That was the end of his would-be son-in-law, but not the end of the story. The glass that was produced that day was used to glaze the windows of the property then known as 22 Colliergate – now the site of The Last Drop Inn. According the story James put out, if you look up at the top window of the pub at night you will see the screaming face of Charles Kimmeridge writhing in the glass, desperate to be re-united with his sweetheart. Should that particular glass ever be broken, the legend has it, the tormented ghoul will be released to haunt the old glazing premises and all the inhabitants therein, in search of his long lost love.

I think it was June 2003 when the president of the International Ghost Research Foundation, Diana Jarvis, visited the brewery and officially presented the Lord Mayor with a certificate proclaiming York the most haunted city in the world. I'm not sure whether she had heard James' story, but she did organise a Ghost Squad to stay in the brewery overnight with their equipment. They saw no centurions, but did claim to have encountered an old gent from the Victorian era who came up from the brew-house to the bar door, peered through the window and shook his fist before disappearing downstairs shouting. They said his name was Ebenezer. I suggested he might be a local fancying a late night beer, but Diane Jarvis was adamant: he was 'from the other side'.

Julie had a friend, Don Nixon, a steward at York City's supporters' club who bought in Terrier on match-days. One day he phoned and said the club was trying to smarten up crumbling Bootham Crescent. He asked whether I fancied footing the bill for re-painting the water tower, in exchange for which we could have our name on it. I immediately hired a sign-writer who transformed the ageing structure into a high-visibility billboard that exposed our name to a few thousand every home game – and still does. We supported a rescue campaign when the club got into trouble in 2002, creating a Save City ale and donating 10p for every pint sold. Add the odd match-ball and we can claim we did our bit for the Minstermen, as they call themselves – although I did wonder whether the Church of England might come gunning for them as they did us.

Sponsorship is a great way of getting your name out there, but it can go horribly wrong. Chaddy, the T-shirt guy, was a member of 'Ales Angels', a group of regulars at the Blue Bell on Fossgate, whose landlords were the affable Jim and Sue Hardie. Each year Jim would organise some sort of adventure for charity. They cycled across Ireland; biked from London to Paris; paddled canoes on Lake Windermere, and rowed a lifeboat from Scarborough to Whitby. The odd thing about this was that to look at Chaddy you'd think the only exercise he ever got was walking his dog to the pub and back. In 2002 they were let down by regular sponsors and asked if York Brewery would pick up the baton. They were to row a lifeboat along the Thames as part of the Queen's Golden Jubilee celebrations. I agreed to put up £1,000, so long as we had exclusivity. So I wasn't too pleased when I picked up my copy of *The Publican* to see a photograph of my crew under Westminster Bridge wearing Theakstons T-shirts. But it's hard to stay cross with the Jims and Chaddys of this world – especially when they revealed that the lads from Masham had thrown a bundle of cash their way. As they said, handing me a complimentary pint, 'It's all for a good cause, right?'

17.
'THAT'S THE BEST GAG
I'VE HEARD TONIGHT'

We now had a liquor licence allowing us to serve drinks until midnight. That meant that we could advertise party nights – which we did, sending out letters to a load of local businesses: *In business, if you are standing still you are going backwards...* 'Has anyone ever said you couldn't organise a piss-up in a brewery? Now's your chance to prove them wrong.'

The response was good, and word spread like a bush-fire. With the help of White Rose Catering we put on some cracking nights out. For music we got a former colleague of my ex-wife, an English teacher from Archbishop Holgate school who ran a disco at the Cock and Bottle. Julian Hird never complained about lugging all his gear up our stairs, he always showed up, and he got everybody dancing.

Of course we got complaints, nearly all of them from one

miserable sod whose house fronted onto Micklegate and backed onto us. He wrote several letters to the Council, claiming that we were a noise nuisance, and we did our best to please him. We installed double-glazing in the windows – which meant the place got hotter than hell and we had to install air conditioning. We had several visits from the 'noise man', who declared that the levels were perfectly acceptable for a city centre venue before midnight. But still our neighbour complained. One time he phoned me while the disco was going full bore. I couldn't resist it. 'Sorry,' I shouted. 'Can't hear you. Way too noisy in here. You'll have to call back in the morning.'

When you have a runaway success such as we were having you soon start to believe you really can walk on water. Not so, sadly. We had a visit from a couple of guys who had started up a comedy club and were looking for a new venue. Comedy was really taking off at that time – the new rock `n` roll and all that. Sure, I said, let's do it. We decided to book them in on the last Sunday of the month. Over the first three gigs we started to build a regular audience. For the fourth the place was packed. Then they booked a trio of comedians who just lacked that certain something. Let me put it another way. They weren't funny. I soon had the first complaint. 'Steady on,' I said, 'I don't book the acts. I just provide the venue. Anyway, what do you expect for three quid? Bob Hope?' 'That's the first decent joke I've heard tonight,' he said.

Still, the comedy adventure lasted longer than our jazz nights, the brain-child of Albert Pattison, a team-mate of mine at Rowntrees C.C. He had an amazing collection of jazz records. Come eight o'clock Albert and I were at the bar, waiting for the punters to show up. And waiting. And waiting. They came eventually – one couple, both brewery club members. After a while the guy asked, 'Can't we have a change?' 'Course not,' I said. 'This is Jazz Night.' 'Really?' he replied. 'Can't stand the bloody stuff.' And with that the pair of them drank up and left.

Otherwise, we were doing well, brewing fifty to sixty barrels a week and the bottling side of the business was taking off too. Centurion's Ghost Ale was getting a lot of plaudits among the cognoscenti and we knew we had to get it into bottles. The supermarkets would surely fall over themselves to stock it – although if they did we would need to expand our capacity further. The solution was another twenty-barrel fermenter which, with a bit of jiggery-pokery, we were able to fit into an extended fermenting room. David Smith was in attendance for the installation, and he advised us to put in an extractor fan to remove additional carbon dioxide that would be created. We did as he suggested, and fitted it so that it discharged into the gap between us and the building next door, a driveway into the back of an Indian restaurant.

One day as I walked into the brewery I saw this guy looking out of the gallery window. 'Can I help you?' I asked. He replied that he was a builder and had applied for planning permission to erect some flats on the land between us. I thought nothing more about it until I got a letter from his solicitors. They advised us that, since we were pumping air into their client's air space, we needed to negotiate either a one-off payment or arrange a weekly rent. I knew what my answer would be, but consulted our legal team first. They agreed on a two-word response, but a more polite one than I had in mind. It read, 'Nice try'.

There aren't many men who can justifiably claim that calling in at the pub on their way home is all part of their day's work. As much as I was tied up at the brewery, I made a point of visiting the Last Drop whenever I could. I walked in one evening, greeted the bar staff and settled down with

my pint and the evening paper. I hadn't been there many minutes when a large, dishevelled woman in her thirties came in and started pestering customers for money. Neither James nor Vernon were on duty so I decided that, as Managing Director, it was my responsibility to tackle her. As politely as I could, I asked her to leave.

The look she gave me would have stopped a runaway train. It was quite chilling. She seemed to be weighing up her options – to glass me, knee me in the balls or take me outside and give me a good going-over. To my surprise and relief, she smiled sweetly and walked out. The customers congratulated me, and I resumed my seat, feeling rather pleased with my display of calm assertiveness. The good feeling lingered for about forty-eight hours, at which point I got a call from James.

'Tony, they're telling me you asked a lady to leave the other night.' 'Yes,' I said, and waited for him to tell me how much he appreciated my efforts. 'Don't you ever read the *Press*?' he asked. 'I mean, do you know who she was?' 'Not the faintest. Should I?' He paused, then gave me her name, which I'd better not repeat. 'She's always in the paper,' he added. 'What for?' 'Drunkenness, violence, anti-social behaviour. She's seriously dangerous. She came back here last night and I had to call the police.' 'Really? What happened?' 'Right, the first cop was six-foot three, sixteen stone.' 'And?' 'And she flattened him. Classic right upper-cut. He was flat on his back.' 'Strewth.' 'Right, so the reinforcements came in. Three of them.' 'Big lads?' 'Bigger than the horizontal one. Combined weight about fifty stone.' 'And they sorted her out, right?' 'They got her as far as the back of the paddy-wagon, and she just stood in the doorway, hands up, daring them to try anything.' 'Hell fire.' 'Anyway, the lad she'd laid out joined in and between them they got her in. So you were a lucky fellow, Tony. She could've had you for breakfast.'

James was doing a terrific job at The Last Drop. He'd adopted Frank Cartin's strategy, joining in rounds with customers who felt obliged to reciprocate and generally spent the rest of the evening in the place. The advantages of having our own outlet were really starting to hit home. Not only were we finally selling substantial quantities of beer in York, but we were able to make sure it was properly cared for in the cellars – and we always got our casks back. It was win, win, win. As more locals sampled our beer other pubs, finding that their customers were voting with their feet, started putting in orders with us. There was a real synergy between the pubs and the brewery: increased numbers of tourists were coming through and, because we were also retailers we had suppliers wanting us to sell their products.

Chris Holmes and I were getting along well and when I couldn't track him down I invariably spoke with his excellent commercial director, Colin Wilde. It wasn't long before we were able to start drawing monies from the business to ease our cash-flow. If one thing was now glaringly obvious it was that we could do with another pub.

Never under-estimate the importance of contacts. I'd been on friendly terms for some time with the restaurant manager of Plunkett's, a pricy but classy place in High Petergate, just inside the city walls in the shadow of Bootham Bar. His name was Simon Wallis. Apart from the fact that I liked the guy, he was a close friend of Mark Hepworth, the solicitor with Denison Till who had handled my divorce and looked after any licensing issues at the brewery. I valued Simon's opinions, so when he took me aside one day and asked, 'You're not by any chance thinking of opening another pub in town, are you?' I was all ears.

He told me that the owner of Plunkett's, Trevor Ward, also had a house further up the street, number 15, and wondered whether it had any potential as a pub. I called Trevor next morning. The building in question housed a clothes shop on the ground floor – mainly black leather gear decorated with chains – and a piercing parlour below that. The tenants were on a rolling three-monthly rent. Trevor wanted something more solid – like a twenty-five-year lease.

He took me for a look around, and it was clear that there would be none of the problems we'd had to overcome at the Last Drop: there was plenty of space, especially as Trevor already had planning permission for a conservatory at the rear. In addition, it was a fantastic location, looking across at the Minster. I got onto Chris at Castle Rock. As soon as he saw the place he was keen as mustard.

Striking a deal with Trevor was easy: the guy was an absolute gent – and he didn't waste time. The planning permission and liquor licence were acquired without any major hitches, and it was time for me to do what I liked best: getting stuck into a new venture.

We secured the services of Guy Moorey, the architect we'd worked with on the Last Drop, and he quickly knocked out some drawings for the 'change of use' application. Permission was granted – as was the liquor licence – we were able to proceed. Sally Robinson agreed to cover the legals, and I went back to Adrian Taylor for the building work.

To build the conservatory, Adrian had to excavate the garden to a depth of six feet. On a site as old as this we had to bring the Archaeological Trust in, lest any significant finds showed up. They would have to be logged, boxed and consigned to the York Museum – and we would be responsible for the costs, at £50 a box. Were anything of real value to be found the work would have to be suspended while a full-scale dig was carried out. For a building so close to the Minster and the Roman remains in its undercroft, this was a serious worry. Fortunately, nothing exciting turned up.

Nevertheless, the conversion took time. The builders literally had to wheel-barrow all the excavated earth through the building, up the road to the location set aside for our skip, which was right under the window of the four-star Dean Court Hotel restaurant. It was on a Sunday morning that I received a call from the manager there, David Brooks. 'Tony,' he said, 'sorry to bother you but my customers pay a lot of money for their breakfast – and their Minster view. Only trouble is, they're looking out over their scrambled egg at a skip piled high with rubble, and guess what's perched on top? A mucky old toilet bowl.' 'Ah,' I said. 'I'll get it shifted.'

As the building work proceeded I turned my thoughts to the décor. I did not want a Last Drop Mark 2. I wanted to achieve a much lighter finish and a more modern look, while retaining the building's original atmosphere. Downstairs, I could see, there was ample room for toilets and a proper cellar which had space for as many as nine hand-pulls – more than anywhere I could think of in York, with the possible exception of The Maltings. One unique feature – rather forced upon us by circumstances – was the access to this lower floor. Structurally, there was only room for a very narrow set of stairs, and that had us scratching our heads until Adrian came up with the idea of a spiral staircase. We liked it, and had one made in wrought iron. It would turn out to be a big hit.

We still hadn't come up with a name - or a manager, but James Butler solved that one for us when he put in a transfer request from The Last Drop, leaving Vernon to take over there. As to the name, I decided in the end to run a competition in the *Press*. Most of the ideas that came in were based on The Last something or other, and I didn't like any of them – although I did for a while think about calling it The Last Supper. I soon dropped that: my mother, who was a regular church-goer, was appalled by the idea. I tried to persuade her it was a joke, but she thought it was in very poor taste. We were just a few weeks from opening and still without a name, when Chris Titley wrote a piece in his 'Bar Talk' column.

Remember when Bar Talk revealed that York Brewery's second pub in Petergate was all set to be called the Centurion Inn? It was another Pulitzer Prize-winning piece of investigative journalism. So you will not be surprised that next month the pub will open under the name… The Three Legged Mare. We must thank James Spriggs for the name. He wrote directly to Tony, suggesting the Centurion Inn was 'a little too obvious'.

The Three Legged Mare was the nickname for the three-post Tyburn Scaffold on the Knavesmire. This was a triangular-shaped gibbet allowing multiple hangings, the poor sufferers being seated on the back of a cart, and left hanging when the cart was driven forwards.

For coming up with the name, James wins a year's free membership to the Brewery Club for him and his wife Sally, and an invitation to a VIP opening night.

We will be covering the opening, natch, and the launching of the brewery's third pub, if that ever happens, provisionally titled The Hung, Drawn and Quartered and left on a Spike for Birds to Peck at Inn.

We had a great opening night which went on into the early hours, and the pub's success was staggering, far exceeding our initial targets. As to the name, it didn't take long for the pub to become known locally as The Wonky Donkey. The place perfectly suited James' style and personality and he quickly established it on the circuit. When you've got a great business good staff gravitate towards you, and James had no problem recruiting a first-class team. We were so thrilled with the way things were going that Chris, Colin and the team from Castle Rock agreed with Smithy and me that we should start looking for pub number three. Before we got busy on that, however, we found ourselves unexpectedly involved in another area altogether.

From time to time we had been invited to sell our wares at events. Barbara's husband Pop used his skills as a joiner to make us a mobile bar which we took to a succession of fetes, carnivals, birthday bashes, village hall dances, and events such as the Cycle Show on the Knavesmire.

Smithy and I soon came to the conclusion, however, that they were hardly worth the effort for the relatively small returns. For one thing, they were too reliant on good weather. We resolved that we would only do outside events if they were big enough for us to make a decent profit. Then we got a call from a major eventing company, Warners, who wanted a mobile bar for the Northern Caravan Show, due to run Thursday to Sunday at York racecourse. They were expecting hundreds of caravanners and possibly thousands of visitors.

We set up the little bar in our allocated spot near the site entrance. Things were going fairly well when I asked one of the organisers about the people who'd parked their motor caravans up in the field for three days. There were hundreds of them. What did they get up to in the evenings? 'Follow me,' she said. She took me to an area inside the race course and opposite the main stand where I saw the biggest marquee I'd ever clapped eyes on. 'How many does this hold?' I asked. She told me that generally, when there was a band on, it held 1000 to 1500 at tables – with room to dance; but on the Saturday they set it up theatre style for the big act. 'Then we get two thousand.'

That evening I followed the crowds up to the marquee and watched what happened. I can't remember how many beer pumps there were, but each one was surrounded by a swarm of people. They ran out of stock, glasses and room. Worse still, there was no supervision and everyone was getting hot under the collar. People poured into the marquee, many of them lugging carrier-bags full of cans and bottles.

This was an opportunity if ever I saw one. I went home that evening, wrote up what I'd seen and added some notes on what we would do if we had the contract for the large marquee. Back at the mobile bar I did a major PR job, making sure all the staff told the customers to recommend that the organisers get York Brewery in next year – and to add a few accolades for our staff. It wasn't hard persuading them: they were all relatives of Smithy, shipped in from Leeds.

The following year we were duly invited to tender for the large marquee, and had our bid accepted. We were well prepared. We had bought ten six-foot bars, which enabled us to erect a thirty-foot long bar on either side of the stage. We had plenty of York Brewery staff in their polo shirts, with two hand-pulls and one lager at six-foot intervals. We managed to prevent most of the people from bringing their own booze in, partly by displaying notices warning them that we wouldn't allow it, but equally by not charging inflated prices. Outside, where our casks were all lined up, we hosed them down with water to keep them cool.

We did such a good job that Smithy won contracts at two of the organiser's other shows – Newark and Lincoln. The annual overall profit on these large events was the equivalent of our having another pub. Not that everything went smoothly. When Ken Dodd was performing they stretched the marquee to accommodate 2,500, all seated. We were literally rubbing our hands in anticipation of the money we would make, and had everyone geared up to spring into action when the break came. The only trouble was, Mister Dodd didn't do breaks – a fact well known to everybody except us. Worse than that, he overran to such an extent that when he finally pranced off stage with his tickling stick it was past closing time – and we had to adhere to that or risk losing our licence. Fortunately, Smithy had had the good sense to send out staff with trays, notepads and pens to take orders during the performance; otherwise we would have really caught a cold. I calculated that we lost £6,000 in sales thanks to Doddy's unscheduled overtime. He may have had his audience in stitches; he had us tearing our hair out.

Sunday was the last day of the show and a lot of campers left early, so we knew that the evening would be slow. Smithy, however, had other ideas. He advertised all the beer we had left at a pound a pint – and got rid of the lot, a gesture that saved us time and hassle, and created a great fund of goodwill. He invited all the staff on-site as well as any food or retail vendors and created a party atmosphere. He loved organising this event, and continued to do so for the next ten years. He sometimes hired as many as forty staff – nearly all of them, of course, related to him. Roy was always there too, reading the tills, counting the cash and making sure everybody had enough change. Smithy bought a caravan for himself and his twin sister Angie, his assistant at these events, and a load of tents for anyone who wanted to stay over. It was one huge fiesta, and many a marriage was made – and broken – on Smithy's watch. He was gutted a few years later when York lost the show and it moved briefly to Pickering, thence to Cheshire. Still, he and Angie continued to do a number of others. Running these events properly took an enormous amount of planning and organisational skill, and it's a huge tribute to Smithy that they went so smoothly.

Our events side took us to some unusual venues, like the raves in Dalby Forest where headliners such as Jools Holland, Status Quo, Pulp and Bryan Ferry came over all prima donna. Jools Holland's outfit were amongst the fussiest, demanding that we laid out all their soft drinks by brand, and with the labels facing the same way. They had to have ice-cubes in buckets, champagne and Cuban cigars – with boxes of Swan Vesta matches, plus some obscure brand of vodka for their drummer. Smithy finally tracked it down to an off-licence in Leeds. All worthwhile, if you ask me: the guy played the longest and best drum solo I've ever seen.

You never knew what was coming next. Status Quo's management complained to him that the on-site caterers had let them down. 'What is it they want?' Smithy asked, wearily. 'Beetroot and corned beef sarnies,' he was told. Smithy gave a big grin. 'Guess what I've got in my caravan?' he said.

As we moved into 2002 our sales were holding steady at 60 to 70 barrels a week, and we were finally making a decent profit. The picture would have been a lot healthier, of course, were we not handing over huge dollops of cash to our friends at Customs and Excise.

The Chancellor was taking 40 per cent of the income from sales, month after month, and it hurt. Ever since we set up in 1996 we'd been paid-up members of the Society of Independent Brewers, and supported its campaigns. SIBA was established in 1980 to represent small outfits just such as ours. They had some able and committed people at the top, men like Keith Bott from Titanic Brewery and Nick Stafford from Hambletons. Every year in the run-up to the Budget, SIBA would get us all to write to our MPs urging them to support the idea of a progressive duty on beer which would reduce the burden for us smaller operators. Looking abroad, we were aware that a flat rate discount applied in the USA, encouraging a sharp growth in the independent sector. The European Union had also adopted a progressive beer duty but certain countries, including the UK, had declined to sign up. It sometimes felt as if we were only in business to earn revenue for the Government, and to collect it on their behalf.

I can't say I'd ever been a man of huge political conviction, rather someone who would vote for whichever party seemed to offer the best deal for small businesses – and generally that wasn't Labour. I was amazed, then, in 2002 when Gordon Brown introduced a Progressive Beer Duty, which basically gave a 50 per cent reduction for the first 5,000 hectalitres (approximately 3,000 barrels, or the equivalent of our annual output). Good Old Gordon, as I will always remember him, single-handedly transformed a modestly profitable year into something approaching a bonanza.

We took a look at the magic figure '£200,000' that now

featured in the 'plus' column, wiped the daft grins off our faces, took another look to make quite sure we weren't hallucinating, then went out and spent it. Not on flashy cars for the directors, but on two not-very-old Mercedes Sprinters – much to the delight of our long-suffering draymen. We also invested in a load of new stainless steel casks. And we replaced the cooling jackets to the five fermenters with a system of coils wound around the outside and set in a graphite conductor paste – yet another measure designed to ensure the quality of the beer. We invested in staff development too, paying Andrew his expenses as he went on a series of 'hop walks' with our suppliers Farams in the hop-fields of Slovenia and the USA. Andrew had originally joined us as a keen amateur brewer, although one we respected one hundred per cent. He'd unquestionably repaid our trust in him, many times over. Once his beers started winning prizes he decided he ought to get some qualifications to go with his growing reputation. He studied hard and passed a succession of tough written exams covering raw materials, microbiology and engineering, and in 2000 got his Institute of Brewing Associate Certificate. The guy awarding it was the chairman of the Institute's Yorkshire and North Eastern section, none other than our consultant David Smith. Perhaps the toughest challenge Andrew faced in the entire process was being forced to drink Tetley's at the Institute's AGM – although he somehow mustered the generosity of spirit to describe the beer as 'becoming more consistent', a clear sideswipe at Carlsberg, who had taken over Tetley's as recently as 1998. The day after that ceremony Andrew came to work, dog tired, and decided to have a quick nap on the malt sacks. My daughter Tessa was leading a tour party that day, and when she paused in the grain store to ask whether there were any questions, some bright spark said, 'Aye, who's that asleep

down there?' 'That gentleman,' Tessa answered, 'is our award-winning head brewer – and he's been out celebrating a very prestigious award, so let's not disturb him.'

Recognition also came Andrew's way when he was voted onto the northeast committee for SIBA. Such high office required him to talk to the press and broadcast media in an official capacity, and he soon became a polished interviewee and spokesman. We decided around this time that Andrew and Nick really could do with a dedicated office. There was a room upstairs, next to the grain store, which housed an old, defunct boiler. Once we'd ripped that out and splashed a bit of paint around they had a spacious and pleasant work-space.

So, we had happy draymen, happy brewers and now we turned our attention to the board. How do you put a smile on a director's face? It's quite easy, really: you pay off a few loans at the bank.

18.
OFF WITH HIS HEAD!

The pubs were going great, their appeal broadened by a few other breweries' products. Obviously we sold Castle Rock's, and we were keen to add a beer from any other microbrewery which had its own pub outlet. We would take six firkins from them, send them six of ours, and as they were emptied each party would fill them with their own brew and switch over – a perfect example of reciprocal trading.

We also had stocked some more exotic beer in bottles – particularly Belgian brews such as Timmermans' Strawberry, Lindemans' Framboise, and Liefmans. Many of these foreign brewers would send us fancy glasses, immediately targetted by trophy-hunters. These people were particularly drawn to a beautiful glass with its own stand offered by Kwak. After some thought, James at the Three-Legged Mare came up with a novel solution to the problem. Anyone ordering a bottle of this brew had to surrender his or her right shoe, to be given back in exchange for the empty glass and stand. With such a line-up of beers on offer we decided to print our own beer menu, much like the wine list you'd be given in a restaurant. It included tasting notes and a few lines on the brewery and place of origin. It cost us, but was well worth it – and we were pretty sure that ours were the first to appear in York.

Being so close to the Minster, we were well placed to profit from the crowds who gathered outside the west face to see in the New Year. The first year, the Wonky Donkey was packed and James made sure that new arrivals only entered as others left. As midnight approached and people went outside to cheer the bells and kiss total strangers, he issued a re-admission ticket, but only to those he wanted back in after the last strains of Auld Lang Syne echoed down Petergate.

The following year Julie and I were at a fancy-dress do. I went as Scott of the Antarctic, all wrapped up in muffler, fur hat and copious amounts of white stuff sprayed on my eyebrows. Towards midnight we went and joined the crowds outside the Minster. After the bells ringing in the New Year, I lent James a hand at the door. I'd had a few and forgot I was dressed up. Days later, James said the York Arms doorman opposite, waived him over, pointed at me and asked whether he could do with a hand getting rid of "that fucking idiot".

With two pubs doing so well for us, we were soon looking for a third. Chris was hoping to buy a free house, but the only ones I knew in York were the Maltings and Fibbers, neither of which were going to be available any time soon. Much as I disliked the strategies of the large pub companies, I was getting to know – and to like – a business development manager at Enterprise who looked after a lot of pubs in the York and east-coast area, a smashing lady called Delia Ricketts. Delia was a big fan of cask ale, and wanted her tenants to stock more of it. She was very well aware of the benefits – namely, more customers and increased sales.

Enterprise, along with Punch, had introduced schemes which enabled their tenants to order one cask ale from a list of SIBA members' beers put out by their head office – and late in 2001 we had got Terrier on the Enterprise beer of the month list. At this point Delia called me to ask whether we would like to set up a competition around her pubs to raise the cask ale profile. We hatched a scheme and I passed on the details to our friends at Bar Talk – namely that whichever of her pubs ordered the most Terrier between the 17th of December and the 3rd of January could send twenty regulars to the brewery for a two-hour session in which they could drink as much as they wanted. I can't recall who won, but I do know it brought us a lot of new admirers around the Enterprise pub chain.

During one of my conversations with Delia, it became clear that among the several pubs she looked after there was one that was languishing. The Queen in Lawrence Street, just outside the city walls, seemed unloved – except by the travelling community who occupied a nearby site. Drawn by its pool table, juke-box, dart-board and cheap lager, they had recently clasped the place to their collective bosom. The pub's regulars slowly drifted away, and there were regular police visits to sort out disturbances. I asked Delia what the average weekly takings were. She seemed embarrassed. 'A few hundred,' she said. I told her she must surely have better things to do than try to chase a lost cause. 'You're right,' she said, 'but where am I going to find someone crazy enough to take it off my hands?' 'How about the Mildly Mad Pub Company?' I said. It took two weeks for Enterprise's estates office to realise I wasn't joking, or mildly

Opportunities might turn up out of the blue – the trick is to spot and grab them...

216

mad, and agree to part company with the freehold for the modest sum of £140,000. I immediately arranged to meet Chris on site, where we discussed the pros and cons.

The first worry was the three pubs in close proximity, The Waggon and Horses, the Rose and Crown and the Tam O'Shanter. But that, we decided, shouldn't be a problem. This was an area with a lot of chimney pots and a number of new housing developments in progress. It was also surrounded by student accommodation, and was on the walking route from campus to town. Looking around the actual premises, we were impressed with the potential. There was a bar that could easily be extended, and the cellar was big enough to take a dozen pumps. The building looked solid enough, and when, a few weeks later, a structural survey failed to reveal any major problems I called Delia and told her we could offer £130,000. She did her best to conceal her delight, and told us she'd pass it on to the people who made these decisions.

So far, the incumbent landlady had no idea what was going on. When she heard, she told me that a deputation of her locals wanted to come up to the brewery to talk about our plans. 'What are they worried about?' I asked. She said that they wanted things to stay as they were – and made it plain they'd visited the Last Drop Inn and were not impressed with the idea of their beloved local being turned into a 'fucking boring shithole with crap lagers'. I explained to her that we were an independent player, free to do as we saw fit, and that we would apply the same principles to the Queen as we had to our other pubs. We never heard any more.

As to finding a manager for the new place, both Chris and I agreed that Vernon, from the Last Drop, was the man. He had a very capable deputy, Elaine, and she had just got engaged to a very personable Aussie lad called Dave. They would make an ideal team to take over from Vernon.

P*** Up In A Brewery

We now took a closer look at the premises and called in our old chum Adrian Taylor. We weren't looking for a massive amount of work: a bar extension, a canopy outside, new windows and a general make-over. Before he started stripping the place, I had a chance conversation with one of our members who used to be a regular at the Queen. He wanted to know whether I'd had a look at the floor. 'No,' I said, 'it's carpeted over. Is there a problem?' He explained that there was, as he recalled, a rather splendid mosaic. 'Looks like marble,' he said. I went back to the pub, bought a pint and casually lifted a corner of the carpet with my foot when nobody was looking. It was pristine, just waiting to be cleaned up and revealed to our new customers in all its glory. I should add that I never finished the pint. It was horrible.

Building work done, the place needed a proper clean-up. We drafted in a world-class outfit – Smithy's cousins and his sisters and his aunts. They soon had the toilets gleaming, kitchen sparkling, then tackled two upper floors used as overnight accommodation in the distant past. Among the delights they uncovered behind the radiators and under the carpets were dozens of used condoms.

We were soon back to scratching our heads over a new name. Our decision to ditch 'The Queen' in Jubilee Year was seized on with a glad cry by our friendly columnist in his Bar Talk slot. 'How dare he?' he ranted. 'And in this most royal of years, to boot? Send him to the Tower! Off with his head! In what can only be described as a deliberate snub to Her Glorious Majesty, York Brewery's Tony Thomson is to rob this royal city of its Queen. Disloyal Tony is to give The Queen on Lawrence Street… a new name! And he has no intention of renaming it Good Queen Lilibet. So what is he going to call it? The President Blair? Alas, Tony hasn't thought of anything, so it's over to you.'

We ran another competition, offering a prize of free club membership, a case of beer and an invitation to the VIP opening night. The winner – who clearly knew a thing or two about unusual monickers – was Margaret Chicken. And the name she came up with? The Rook and Gaskill. Her suggestion was based on a double execution on May 1st 1676, when two felons were hanged from the gallows outside Walmgate Bar, barely a stone's throw from our new pub.

We needed a stand-out sign and hired Alex Curzon of Sign Arts in Bishopthorpe. We also went back to our friends David Hulme and son Daniel, who rummaged through their warehouse in Tadcaster and dug out some excellent furniture. They must have missed the chairs they sold us, because they regularly showed up as customers. David was planning to retire and hand over the business to his son. It wasn't to be. Tragedy struck when Daniel went on a ski-ing holiday and was killed by an avalanche. How David held himself together during a heart-rending eulogy at the funeral service, I have no idea. It certainly was something I'll never forget.

The R and G, as it was soon known, had a grand opening. Kevin with new wife Carol was in fine form. It was great to see him again. One delightful outcome was that my dear friend Alice finally found her Mister Right in Castle Rock's Commercial Director – later Managing Director – Colin Wilde. I introduced them, they started chatting, and have been together ever since.

The pub was launched. Staffed by people who knew about the products they sold and kept them in tip-top condition, it soon attracted a decent evening crowd of regulars, people who appreciated proper beer and pleasant surroundings. As to the previous customers, they came to look at the improvements and decided the new look wasn't for them. They took their custom elsewhere.

19.
ON TOP OF THE WORLD

It was April 2002 when Andrew, Nick and myself, put on our best suits and York Brewery ties and boarded the train to Kings Cross. Arriving there, we took a taxi to the Guildhall. We were heading to one of the most prestigious events in the trade calendar, the Brewing Industry International Awards, and we were calmness personified. We were under no pressure whatsoever. We'd done fantastically well to get Centurion's Ghost Ale to the finals and were thus guaranteed a medal. This was a chance to sit back, tuck into the free food, have a few glasses of quality ale, and pat ourselves on the back.

Entering the hall, we were shown into a smart suite of conference rooms where the results of the judging were to be projected onto a large screen. We were competing with two beers, 1859 Porter from Harvey & Sons of Lewes and Flanagan's Dry Irish Stout from the Townville Brewing Co., whose head brewer had travelled from Australia for the event.

When the medals were announced I really couldn't take in what I was seeing. The stout was awarded bronze, the porter got silver, and York's own Centurion's Ghost... gold. We would now contest the prize of Champion Beer in our category, which was Dark Mild, Stout and Porter.

Still somewhat dazed, we went and sank a couple of pints before going into the dining room. The place was enormous. Every table was loaded with jugs of beer, bottles of wine, port and whisky. I wish I could remember what I ate, because I know it was superb, but the fact is I haven't the faintest recollection. I do know that there was a lot of it and that lunch took a long, long time, during which we made serious inroads into the beer and wine, followed by a couple of fine malts – and that I was congratulating myself, when the cheeseboard came around, on having declined the port. Win, lose or draw, I wanted to be fully conscious when the results were announced.

When they finally called the winner, the champion beer in our category, I hardly heard a word of it, just the magic phrase, 'From York Brewery... Centurion's Ghost Ale!' Andrew, Nick and I were left open-mouthed, staring at each other. Reflecting from this distance, I can see quite clearly that it was a high point in my life and as such ought to be etched in my mind in vivid detail. Trying to put pictures to the memory, I have to admit defeat. I remember next to nothing, only someone saying one of us had better approach the platform to accept the award and deliver a few words. No way was this my job. Andrew had conceived the brew, perfected the profile of taste and flavour. He refined the recipe. Then he and Nick had tweaked it – more than once, gradually upping the ABV from 5.0 per cent to 5.4 per cent. My contribution? The name.

So Andrew went to take the laurels. He spoke rather well, I thought, considering he was facing 600 guests, including several titans of the brewing industry, and had consumed even more alcohol than I had. He came back to the table with the biggest grin on his face, lugging our trophy. It was a beautifully polished wooden 'pin', or four-and-a-half gallon cask. They'd put a metal plate on it, inscribed with the our names. It was a handsome trophy, and one we would treasure throughout the time we held it.

The spin-offs were immense. Firstly, sales rose sharply. Wetherspoons, headline sponsors, ordered Ghost for all their pubs during the various festivals over the next few months. And all our wholesalers demanded it for their beer of the month promotions. Bottled sales were also affected as supermarkets and the large off-licence chains sought to get on the bandwagon. For the first time we now regularly brewed to capacity, which was 100 barrels a week, or 30,000 pints.

Success hadn't come overnight; it had taken six years of unremitting hard graft, and now I was looking back to the days when I used to say to Smithy, 'Think of it as a journey, an adventure, a trip to savour and enjoy. You should relax and enjoy it.' Smithy answered that as only Smithy would. 'Practise what you fucking preach then.'

Looking back, I can see that we'd both been feeling the long hours and incessant worry. In November 2002 Julie and I arrived at Leeds-Bradford airport after spending a week in Gran Canaria. When I switched my phone on I saw that I had a message to call my daughter Emma, urgently. I immediately thought that my Dad, who'd been quite ill, had passed away, and when Emma answered my call her voice told me I wasn't far off: someone had died. It wasn't my father, however; it was my mate Kevin. He'd gone to the gym with his wife Carol and collapsed while on a rowing machine – the cause, a massive heart attack. He died instantly, aged 51. He'd been a great friend, an integral figure in the birth of York Brewery, and he'd gone far, far too early. I miss him to this day.

In 2003 I was approached by *The Press* to enter for their Small Business of the Year Award, which was open to all firms within their circulation area. I was reluctant, mainly because they wanted me to submit a 2,500-word script outlining why I should win. If we were short-listed I would be required to show the judges around the place. If selected for the final stage, I would be grilled by said judges and asked to provide evidence to support my answers. It sounded like a lot of hard work, but I gritted my teeth and did as I was asked, reminding myself that all publicity is good publicity. When I told the judges how much the visitors liked our tours they wanted to see the evidence. Fortunately I'd kept all the guest-books and could show that about half of our visitors wrote in them, and were nearly always complimentary.

In due course I got a letter saying that we were one of three finalists in our category and as such were invited to the awards dinner, to be held in the Ebor Suite, York racecourse. It was to be quite an up-market event, and the organisers were giving us free tickets. No, I'd misread that: one free ticket. Guests would pay £80. Smithy and I thought it over and decided, what the hell, we'd take the whole gang, all full-time staff who were available, even if it did cost £1,500. The only person notably absent was Nick, our assistant head brewer. He'd been head-hunted by Timothy Taylor – not that he stayed long in Keighley. Within a year he was back, was tired of pressing buttons and wearing a white coat.

When the big night came it was a shock to see our motley crew decked out in their evening suits, bow ties and party frocks. We made quite an entry and occupied two tables – comfortably outnumbering any other business. We were also the rowdiest – although they had no idea just how noisy we could be until they announced us as the winners.

I was on a roll, it seemed, and should clearly have been on the look-out for a change of fortune. It soon came. After a lifetime of smoking eighty cigarettes a day – Senior Service and Players untipped – my father's health had been declining for some time and his chest was now in a sorry state. To tell the truth it was something of a relief to the family when he finally passed away late in December 2003.

A few weeks later Julie asked me if I was free to come for dinner at the Hazelwood Castle Hotel, out on the A64. I agreed, but failed to notice the date she'd picked. Smithy did, and immediately started whistling 'I'm Getting Married In The Morning'. That's when he pointed out that we were down for February 29th, the day that comes around every four years when, according to tradition, a woman may propose to a man – which Julie did, catching me off-guard as I was trying to

Winning awards will bring extra sales – so enter them always...

make sense of the wine list. She was clearly counting on a positive reply, because she'd provisionally booked the same place for the wedding. They have a chapel out there, and a piece of woodland where the bluebells - her favourite bloom – are thick on the ground. So we would be married in May the following year.

The Press loved it, of course. They ran a story under the headline 'Leap Into Marriage', and a picture of us behind the bar at the brewery. Of course, they had to assure their readers that Julie had fallen for my cask ale, rather than me. Centurion's Ghost was always her favourite.

Things were looking up once more, and the Rook had just been named Town Pub of the season by CAMRA when Smithy decided to put a spanner in the works. Julie and I were about to go abroad. We were planning to take my mother over to Agistri, the Greek island where her sister, my aunt Eve, lived. But with Smithy in charge, everything at Toft Green would be in good hands.

Smithy had always smoked and enjoyed an odd fry-up, about five times a week on average. And apart from his brief stint as a drayman he didn't really get any exercise. As for drink, he worked in a brewery. So was it any wonder that he collapsed in a heap one day, suffering from a massive heart attack? Luckily for him, partner Trevor was dialling up an ambulance before he hit the ground. I shot up to Durham, where I found Smithy in a hospital bed with wires attached and computer screens lit up with zig-zag lines – better than flat ones, he pointed out – not a cigarette or a bottle to be seen. After I'd berated him for the lengths he'd gone to just to get out of working for a living, I suggested that now wasn't a bad time to give up smoking. Then I went outside with Trevor to get the low-down. He told me Smithy's condition was fairly serious but that, in his professional opinion, he expected him to make a full recovery. It would just take time. 'What's your best guess?' I asked. He reckoned six months.

Back at Toft Green I got all the staff together and told them. The mood was sombre for a while, but that didn't last. As soon as Smithy could handle a phone he was on it day and night, puffing on a cigarette and ensuring that Roy and Barbara were up to speed on this or that item, and had they made that call, completed those returns, checked those figures – oh, and what was the latest on sales?

Business was booming, and with the jump in capacity we needed help in the brew-house. Andrew and Nick had got to know a chap called John Buckle who lived locally and had just finished working at John Smith's in Tadcaster after twenty years, the last ten as Laboratory Manager. Wishing to take on a less stressful role, JB joined the team. John was well known around York – as I discovered when I had our pub managers in for a meeting. I was at the table when Andrew and Nick filed in, followed by John. The managers all looked at each other, then at me, then at John.

'What's up?' I asked. 'What's this bloke doing here?' James asked 'John?' I said. 'He's just joined us in the brew-house. Why, do you guys know each other?' 'Know him?' James said. 'I should say so. We've banned him from all the York Brewery pubs.' 'Why?' 'Because as soon as he gets a couple of pints down him he bursts into song.' He looked at John and nodded. 'Great guy,' he said, 'but he gets right up everyone's nose. Has them leaving in droves.'

John was never any trouble to us. His knowledge, experience and expertise were a great help in ensuring the smooth running of the fermenting, conditioning and racking rooms, right up until his retirement in 2015.

Our business was about to undergo a major shift. Chris and I had been talking about the next Mildly Mad pub and wondering where we would find a suitable premises. Barry Crux, a York estate agent, came up with Mowbray's. It was on Stonegate, a wonderful seventeenth-century town house with a glorious tiled façade. It had been operating as a licensed café that sold seriously good ice-cream. When we viewed, however, Chris cooled to the idea. Too small.

Chris and I were already having differences of opinion at the time over the Rook and Gaskill. He wanted to turn it from a managed to a tenanted house. Then there was the old Pizzaland place, latterly the Rock Café, which had been closed for a couple of years by this time and was falling into disrepair. Mice and rats had moved in, there was dust everywhere and the place looked an absolute mess.

Downstairs, at street level, it had a floor area almost as big as the brewery, so it certainly had potential as another pub. Upstairs it had some fifteen rooms on three levels connected by a maze of corridors. The brewery was running out of space and it was clear that if we could acquire the rest of the building we would have enough room to expand the production area, raising our potential weekly output. Such a move would, we felt, safeguard our long-term future. However, if we wanted to convert part of the old café into another pub, there was a fly in the ointment. York Brewery would be the sole tenant for the building, and that would mean that the Mildly Mad pub company, my joint venture with Chris, would be paying rent to the brewery (me). Chris saw that as a conflict of interests – and I couldn't blame him.

Opoortunities come once a business is successful – make the most of them...

Chris and I had made giant strides together, but we realised that these were differences which weren't going to be resolved easily. When he told me that he flat out didn't want to get involved with the Mowbray's project we knew we had reached the end of the road. This sort of thing happens in business, and we both accepted it. We were determined not to fall out over it. Chris wanted the Rook & Gaskill, which suited me. I wanted to hang onto the city centre pubs. They both had twenty-five year leases and the synergy with the brewery, slap bang in the city centre, meant that it made perfect sense for them to remain York Brewery pubs. So we agreed that the Mildly Mad Pub Company would be left as a 'sleeping business' with a token tenner in its bank account. Chris and I worked through this scenario, making notes on the proverbial back of an envelope. Then the lawyers got hold

of it, farted around for six months and produced a folder full of fancy documents, tucked into which was an invoice for several grand. I was reminded of an exchange I'd heard in a pub a few years previously: 'What do you call it when you have a bunch of lawyers chained to a rock at the bottom of the sea?' 'I don't know. Tell me.' 'A fucking good start.'

I had to explain to a lot of people over the next year or so that this was an amicable divorce, and I know many of them simply didn't believe me. But Chris and I are still good mates today and often have a few beers together when Julie and I visit him on the Isle of Man, where her Dad and her twin sister live.

I now forged ahead with the Mowbray venture. The incumbent leaseholders were keen to vacate, but we needed a pub licence, permission for a change of use, and, as we no longer had the benefit of Castle Rock's very agreeable bankers, we needed our own bank to lend us something in the region of £200,000 to fund the conversion works. But hey, that wouldn't be a problem – would it?

Well, it was. The same bank whose Regional Director, Peter Lobb, had presented us with the Small Business of the Year Award twelve months previously made seriously heavy weather of our request. Our new manager, Robert, was very affable but, he explained, the loan I wanted was way outside the limits of his authority. He would have to make a case to his Board, which, with our ever-increasing sales (over £1.5 million a year) and decent profits, shouldn't be an issue. Satisfied that this was going to be a shoo-in, I turned my attention to obtaining the licence and planning consent.

There were a few problems to overcome. Stonegate is a shopping street, and we had to agree to maintain a retail outlet on the ground floor with the bar behind it. There was a further glitch when I met the Conservation Officer on site. He looked at my plans to knock down the toilets in the yard and create a conservatory, and told me that the loos might well have historic value. I couldn't help myself. I laughed out loud. I said, 'If that's the situation I'm ready to call it a day.' To be fair, he compromised. He told me that if planning permission was granted and he came by to find that the toilets had indeed been knocked down he was pretty sure he would've forgotten they ever existed.

In July 2004 our plans were finally approved. That was when Robert, our bank manager, told us that his Board had considered our loan application and wanted more information and more security. For Smithy and me, having already signed our houses to the bank three times over, this was a bridge too far. Considering our financial success to this point we were first gob-smacked, then plain livid. In fact, Smithy, who had barely got over his cardiac arrest, was incandescent – to the point where I genuinely feared that he might have another.

In the end we told Robert he could whistle for his

further security, that we were going to take our debts and loan application where they would be appreciated. At the time, of course, we hadn't any idea where, but it had to be said. There's only so much you can take.

I'd been hearing good things about HSBC, so they were our first port of call. Their Business Development Manager, Angus Woodcock, had a look around the brewery, scanned our latest figures and promised a quick decision. Within a few days he offered us a loan of £140,000, a better deal for all our banking arrangements – and, if we cared to call in, the documents were all drawn up and ready for us to sign. Finally, everything was lined up and we were able to get started on our next venture.

Perseverance is a valuable asset in business, just as it is in life...

We started on the alterations with the aim of being up and running by Christmas. James at the Three-Legged Mare had asked if he could manage the place, and we'd agreed. As ever, the *Press* were right behind us. On December 11th 2004, the Bar Talk columnist proclaimed that, having been well behaved all year, he was being granted his Christmas wish, a lovely new pub. 'The Yorkshire Terrier,' he wrote, 'is set to open on Monday. It is another clever and thoughtful conversion of an ancient building.' He went on to praise the décor and highlight the fact that it sported 'possibly York's only toilet offering a Minster view.'

Our architect, Guy Moorey, and our builder Adrian Taylor were as thrilled as I was when, the following year, CAMRA selected the Terrier as winner of the 'conversion to pub use' category in its Pub Design Awards. This was no minor accolade. The judge was Steven Parissien, Dean of Arts and Professor of Architectural History at the University of Plymouth. 'This year's crop of award winners represent one of the strongest and most eclectic sets of designs it has been our pleasure to announce in over twenty years,' he said.

Attending awards dinners was starting to become a regular occurrence. Smithy and I drove to Bristol with James and his assistant Simon Lucas. It was singularly apt that we should receive a CAMRA award. We owed a debt of gratitude to the York branch, particularly Geoff Henman, for his lobbying on our behalf when it seemed that the planning process was mired in detail. We were becoming very fond of CAMRA for a number of reasons, not least the fact that they now included all three of our pubs in their Good Beer Guide, having just added the Rook & Gaskill. A lot of our brewery club members were also CAMRA people. They often held their monthly meetings with us, and we did tours for groups from all over the country. When CAMRA named the Rook and Gaskill their Pub of the Year in March 2005 we received a fine accolade from Jim Thompson of the York branch. 'When Tony announced that he was taking over the Queens,' he wrote, 'we all thought he was mad. It was a really run-down pub, but they have turned it around. From what was an absolute dive to Pub of the Year. Quite an achievement.'

We always got on well with Jim. When his son Benjamin was born he became, at the age of three weeks, our youngest member. In fact, he'd already done his first brewery tour at the age of five days, and had his christening party in the club bar. So we got to know CAMRA quite well over the years and, by and large, they were supportive. We did have to deal with some odd types. CAMRA members have been compared with train-spotters and even bus-spotters, but when you're an organisation with 75,000 members then and over double that today you have to accept you are a broad church. Or, to put it more bluntly, you will attract a few nutters. Our drayman Richard recalls one landlord who had a baseball bat in a frame over the bar and beneath it the legend 'CAMRA Re-education Tool'. We actually had to ban one or two from the brewery bar, but they were the exception. So, CAMRA: not a bad bunch on the whole, even if one or two members seem to have spent 'too long in the desert'.

With James moving to the Yorkshire Terrier the time seemed opportune for his deputy at the Wonky Donkey, Mandy Pegg, to take up the reins as manager. Mandy had started as a part-timer while still studying English Language and Psychology at York St John. She impressed us so well that we made her deputy manager before she even graduated. She was still only twenty-one, but we were confident she could handle this vibrant and increasingly busy pub. We were fully justified. Mandy did a great job. Bright as a button, with a cheeky manner, she carried on where James left off, and only moved on in 2015 when she was head-hunted by the ambitious Ossett Brewery to run their latest venture, the stylishly refitted Fox Inn on Holgate.

While all the excitement at the Terrier was going on, I was still watching the situation at what used to be Pizzaland and the Rock Café, the area behind the brewery that fronted onto Micklegate. I felt that acquiring the lease for the whole building would be the last piece of a jigsaw. Tragus, who had bought it from Whitbread, still had no real idea that they owned it. I think they'd side-lined it as 'on some street up north somewhere'. So when I suggested we take it off their hands, they were receptive to the idea. All they needed to do was surrender the lease they held with Whitby C Oliver, and leave us to negotiate a new one for ourselves. There were two problems. One, with ten years left on their lease Whitby Oliver Ltd had no real incentive to surrender it. It was money for old rope, a guaranteed rent from a national organisation. Two, Tragus knew that they would be liable to fork out for a whole list of dilapidations - standard practice in such cases. In this case, nothing had been spent on the building in years. The roof, the windows, the guttering, the plasterwork and general décor were all in a very poor state of repair. So Tragus were in a bit of a fix. They wanted out of the lease, but didn't want to be lumbered with a whopping great repair bill. Yet the longer they left it, the worse the situation would become. Aware that we already had a good relationship with the landlords, they concluded that the way forward was to get rid of the lease to us.

Oliver's solicitor was a fellow we had already locked horns with, someone who had frustrated us in the past with delays over what looked to us like minor technicalities. This time, however, he seemed a little more approachable. Every bit as finicky, but less abrasive. The main characters involved in all this were the M.D. of Whitby Oliver Holdings Ltd, a Mr Robert Walker, and their main shareholder Mr Charles Oliver. When we first moved into Toft Green I had met and dealt with Charles' father Donald, a real gent of the old school type. He had since passed away. Charles was different. Whenever I met him he seemed to be with a different woman, always ravishingly beautiful. He certainly enjoyed a beer or two, and often popped into the brewery after attending York races with another glamorous female on his arm.

Charles and Robert were happy with our proposal, which was to negotiate a new 30-year lease as tenants for the whole site at an initial rent of £70,000 a year. Tragus assigned a building company from Leeds to draw up a dilapidations schedule and give me a copy. When it arrived I found myself looking at a file two inches thick. We had a huge interest in seeing that the repairs were thorough since, as soon as the lease was signed, the responsibility for the building fell to us. The builder's foreman confided that Tragus were going to have to shell out £300,000.

We watched as they replaced and repaired the roofs, windows and guttering, re-plastered huge expanses of walls and ceilings. They then ripped out the old electrical system and updated it – right the way through to, and including, the brewery, before re-decorating throughout, internally and externally. The whole premises looked as new as you can expect of a building that has stood for three and a half centuries. No leaks anywhere, all spick and span – and no rodents to be seen. Along with this hugely expanded premises, of course, came the hugely expanded rent – which we couldn't afford.

With the business doing so well, Smithy and I were slowly reducing the hours we put in. We no longer had to work behind the bar and conduct the tours, having employed a full-time manager for the visitor centre. Jan McDermont was a Geordie lass, great at entertaining the tourists and developing the party nights. So we were now starting to put in the kind of working day that people imagine you enjoy when it's your own business, coming in at ten and winding up around four – although I did tend to hang about in the bar sharing a pint or two with the brewers and discussing the finer points of the production side. There followed a leisurely progress back to my little house in Hull Road. Leaving work, I'd call in at the Three-Legged Mare, although not before popping into the Maltings. Sometimes I went for a quick one in the Last Drop, and it was never easy to pass the Blue Bell without calling in for a chat with Jim. Meltons Too had also opened on Walmgate and was selling our beer, so they deserved an occasional visit as well. My final port of call would be the Rook and Gaskill, just ten minutes from home. So there were nights when I was getting back at midnight, fumbling around for my keys, a little the worse for wear but feeling very cheerful. In the long run I'm sure such a routine would have affected my health, although at the time I told myself I was reasonably fit, playing squash two or three times a week – and doing a lot of walking, albeit pub to pub.

I found other reasons to call in at the pubs. One of the things we'd always tried to do was to keep an eye on the opposition. Any business needs to do that. So, every few months I'd take all the managers on a tour of our competitors in the city. The first time we did it I was armed with a notebook and pen to collect details of their prices, and a wad of petty cash to pay for refreshments. Despite the fact that we had a lot of fun, we contrived to come up with some good ideas on the basis of what we saw and heard on our pub crawls. We also gathered intelligence. At each pub I got out my little black book and jotted down the prices. Next morning when I opened it up I'd find that, while the first few samples were neatly recorded, the later ones took a bit of deciphering. And even then they didn't make any sense. Thereafter I delegated the job to one of the managers.

Quality people gravitate towards successful expanding companies...

Securing direct ownership of our pubs was turning out to be a good move. Beyond the fact that we were selling our own beer, we had absolute freedom in choosing our suppliers for wines, soft drinks and so on, and could benefit from their discounts. I had always maintained a good relationship with Beer Seller, the largest cask beer wholesaler in the UK, and now it paid off. They had been taken over by one of the large companies and were now wholesaling the full range of pub products under the name T.B.S. Waverley – and were desperate to increase their sales. They were delighted to do a deal that involved them buying mass volumes of our beer into their depots all over the U.K., in return for supplying our pubs with keg products, wines and spirits. This was going to push us to expand our productive capacity. Thank goodness we'd done that deal, taking on the lease of the rest of the brewery buildings and giving ourselves room to grow.

Sam Goldwyn, legendary Hollywood producer, is said to have remarked: 'The harder I work the luckier I get.' I was finding that the more people I got to know the more I was able to make connections and come up with solutions. I'd recently got to know Ian Fozard, managing director and owner of a North Yorkshire pub chain called Market Town Taverns. He was buying a fair bit of our beer for his pubs, which were scattered around Leeds, Wetherby, Harrogate, Otley and Ilkley - but as yet he didn't have a place in York. One day I picked up the phone and asked him why not. 'Oh,' he said, 'it's not for the lack of trying. I just can't find one I like.'

I put it to him that the former Rock Café in Micklegate might fit the bill. I added that I was keen to sublet it to a company that shared our philosophy regarding cask ale. He arranged to visit the site with the woman who handled the food side of his business, Gil Richardson. They took the idea very seriously, even to the extent of spending a few Friday and Saturday nights savouring the Micklegate madness. The Rock Café site, Ian figured, would provide a haven of sanity, offering a convivial atmosphere and serving proper beer. He was going to name the new place Brigantes, after a Celtic tribe who held sway in Yorkshire in pre-Roman times.

We agreed a lease for an area of the premises that would accommodate an average sized pub – and a large meeting room upstairs which could offer buffets. Downstairs was a massive cellar with an easy 'drop' for casks and kegs from the street. The agreed rent accounted for half of the new rent we had to fork out on our new lease, making it a fantastic deal for us. Ian was delighted with his end of the bargain, and we had the added bonus of him agreeing always to have two York Brewery beers on hand-pull: all we had to do was roll the casks through our back door, along the alleyway and in through their back door, barely twenty yards from our racking area.

We put up a dividing wall between our newly extended premises and Brigantes, enclosing a huge new area. Here we built a much larger cask-wash and storage area and a new conditioning room capable of holding five twenty-barrel tanks. The old one became an additional fermenting room. The new set-up also gave us a larger racking space. In preparation for the additional work-load involved in having sole charge of the pubs, we needed extra administrative help, and here Smithy came up trumps when he recruited Martine Geczy. She was very professional, although her somewhat abrasive style when addressing the management caused Smithy to dub her 'Vinegar Tits' – and it says a lot about her character that she embraced her new name with good humour. Once she got started Smithy took her over to Castle Rock's office at Nottingham where they spent a few days getting to grips with the systems we were to use. Then they packaged up all the paperwork and brought the lot back to Toft Green, where Martine effected the smoothest transition from Mildly Mad to York Brewery pubs. Now, thanks to her, we had managed accounts every month, which enabled us to make better informed decisions.

Martine, of course, needed her own space, but that was no longer a problem. Even Andrew, now promoted to

Director of Brewing, acquired a bit of elbow room at last, moving upstairs to join Barbara and Emma in a large office. Despite the Minster view, he was often to be seen at the window below, the suspicion being that he was keeping down the vermin population with a high-powered air rifle. Smithy, Roy and Martine were also able to move into much more spacious accommodation. Smithy was insistent that as M.D. I needed a room of my own. I suspect he wanted to discuss accounts and administrative matters with Roy and Martine without me sticking my nose in. He knew how I hated to get bogged down in detail.

Besides, I had other things on my mind. Julie and I were about to get married, so I did what all bridegrooms-to-be have to do, and organised a stag week. I rounded up twelve mates, and off we went to Aron, in France for a week's golfing. A few weeks later Julie and I, with Smithy doing best man duties, tied the knot and moved into a converted barn on the Haxby road. It was in a pretty dilapidated state and needed a fair bit of attention, when what I really wanted was more time on the golf course.

Julie meanwhile had bought the Coach House hotel on Marygate and was busy with that. Then came one of those glorious moments when

Keep costs down. If you don't need the space, somebody else will...

business and pleasure combined. I got a call from a lovely lady called Hayley who told me that she was managing a restaurant on a new golf-course out at Flaxton, Sandburn Hall. Keen to offer the public locally sourced food and drink, she was planning to sell our beer in the restaurant, which was called Tykes, and the sports bar. We agreed a deal, and I took out a membership of the club, one I hold to this day.

20.
JUST MAKE SURE YOU
COUNT YOUR FINGERS

Despite all these developments, I was feeling stale. I needed another pub project, and I could feel one coming on. Ian Fozard had done a super job converting the Rock Café. After a great opening night, Brigantes settled into a successful pattern of trading, adding a little touch of beer culture to the rough-and-tumble of Micklegate.

Smithy and I had been over to Leeds to look at a couple of sites, one of which was subsequently opened by Sam Moss and Michael Brothwell of Leeds Brewery. They named it The Midnight Bell after one of their own brews. That pub was their gain and our loss. We soon got over the disappointment when we had a call from Simon Hall of Fleurets Pub Estate Agents. He had a property on the Headrow which, he thought, might interest us.

Doctor Okells was owned by a brewery of the same name in the Isle of Man. The firm had a couple of pubs in

Liverpool and just this one in Leeds. Not surprisingly, given the distance from their home base, they were finding it hard to manage, and it was losing money.

Smithy and I didn't announce ourselves, just went in, ordered a pint and pretended we were punters. It had a strained atmosphere. The staff behaved like Americans, fresh off a half-day customer relations course. Being asked 'What are you up to today sir?' and told to 'Have a nice day' is one thing. To have these words uttered by a muscle-bound, tattooed barman wearing silver earrings and speaking with a broad Leeds accent – well, it just seemed odd.

The strange atmosphere made sense after we'd made our interest known. The whole place was run by a family. The manager's son was his assistant; another son was a chef, and a cleaner – who seemed to rack up an extraordinary number of hours – was his wife. Nevertheless, Smithy and I were very impressed with the location, and were certain that we could add character with new furniture and exploiting one or two attractive features, such as the mezzanine area that overlooked the main bar. The pub had an excellent cellar, so with a manager skilled in handling cask ales we would be able to offer a wide range of beer on an ever-changing roster.

We made it clear that if we took the place on we would install our own manager, someone who was young, had an excellent knowledge of cask ale and knew the Leeds scene. Finding such a person wasn't difficult. There was a Wetherspoons just around the corner and one of their duty managers, upon hearing that Okells was about to change hands, offered his services. Dean Pugh was only twenty-two years old, a recent graduate and a total beer fanatic. Smithy and I took to him immediately. When he talked people seemed to shut up and listen to him. It's a rare talent, and one I've always admired. We hired him right away.

Doing the deal with Okells was the easy part. The hard work started with converting the place into a York Brewery pub. Finding a name, however, was no problem. When you stand across the road and look at the building, right at the top you see a life-size statue, in stone, of a man in a frock coat and flanked by a pair of griffins. I made enquiries and found out that it was a likeness of Mister Patrick James Foley, who founded the Pearl Life Assurance company in 1874. The building housed their chambers. Foley was a former Irish politician, who represented Galway and Connemara in the House of Commons in the 1890s. The building itself dated from 1911 and was one of the first in Leeds to be built of Portland stone. It seemed only proper, armed with this knowledge, to re-christen the pub Mister Foley's Cask Ale House. Richard, our drayman, took photos of the statue, and Alex Curzon used them to create a sign to hang outside. Mr Foley became the logo for the sales and marketing material.

We had a lively opening night, the pub crammed with local dignitaries and everybody we could think of who might help promote its name and reputation. We even invited the management of the establishment next door, a pole-dancing club called Wild Cats. They didn't close until four in the morning, so they invited us to pop into the club after we'd seen our guests off home. Julie decided I needed a reward for my endeavours and arranged a private performance for me. There was a twist, however. There I was, enjoying the undivided attention of a very attractive and stark naked dancer, when my loving wife waltzed in and sat down beside me. The quality of the show nose-dived, but the girl still had the brass cheek to ask for another tenner. 'What for?' I asked. She pointed at Julie and said, 'There's two of you.' But to be fair, this was Julie's treat – and she coughed up.

Exploiting Dean's expert knowledge of cask ale, and

his encyclopaedic knowledge of bottled beers from around the world, we put together a terrific drinks menu at Foley's, and its reputation soon spread. Smithy and I, however, felt nervous about having a pub we couldn't walk to from the brewery. We were outside our own comfort zone with this one. We needn't have worried. Sales were strong and the pub soon received its first official accolade, being CAMRA's pub of the season in the summer of 2008.

After the dust had settled on this latest flurry of activity an interesting and, to me, flattering, piece of gossip reached my ears. One of the team that Simon Hall had sent to talk through the deal with me had apparently asked his boss whether I drove a hard bargain. 'Put it this way,' Simon told him, 'after you've shaken hands with Tony, make sure you count your fingers.'

With four pubs to supply and TBS Waverley increasing their orders, we urgently needed to increase our brewing capacity, and did so in 2007, raising it from 100 to 160 barrels a week, the biggest single expansion since we began in 1996. Five new twenty-barrel conditioning tanks, a forty and a twenty-barrel fermenter had to be dropped in by crane, over the brew-house roof and into the back alleyway, where a big hole had been knocked out of an external wall.

With this increase in capacity, it was time to take on another top-class brewer: Alan Hardie. Since completing his degree in Brewing and Distilling in Edinburgh, he had worked at Wychwood, makers of Hobgoblin, and more recently with Bass in Tadcaster. He'd just gained his Master Brewer's qualification from the Institute of Brewers. In September 2016, Alan, after nine years at York Brewery, left to join Andy Herrington, owner of Ainsty Ales as Head Brewer.

We had worked long and hard to build up York Brewery into a thriving, profitable enterprise turning over £3 million a year. When compiling these memories I asked the current head brewer Nick Webster to go through the records and work out just how much beer duty we had paid during the time Smithy and I ran the place: £3.5 million.

The brewery was still a hands-on affair and the buck always stopped with me or Smithy. In addition, we still owed the bank a fair few quid, over £400,000 to be precise. This was no great worry: we knew we could pay it back pretty quickly out of profits if we chose to do so. We were also aware that if we had a few more pubs we could soon render ourselves virtually bomb-proof, safe from the predators constantly on the look-out for small fish to gobble up. But to get there we would need a massive injection of cash.

So we tested the water. We fed hints to the *Press* and started talking with a company called Avondale, who specialised in brokering deals for small and medium sized businesses. Ideally, we were looking for a local businessman to put up a substantial sum of money for a share of the company, enabling us to build up the estate of pubs. Nobody rose to the bait. Letting go wasn't as easy as it sounded.

Enter Mitchells Hotels and Inns, a family firm based in Lancaster. They had a turnover of £12 million and employed 380 people. Jonathan and Andrew Barker, in their thirties, had recently bought out several other members of the family and now wanted to expand the pub estate in Yorkshire and get back into brewing; music to our ears. So long as they made us an acceptable offer we would be happy to sell – and they did. Their accountants and solicitors were downright rude but the deal went through eventually. I'm often asked for my views on how things have progressed. There are positives. The new owners have 'stretched' our forty-barrel fermenter, raising its weekly capacity from 160 to 180 barrels. They have installed a new machine to speed up the racking procedure, and have rented a warehouse nearby, and did an impressive job re-branding the brewery. Some great new beers have been brewed. A surprising move came when the brewery went into keg production – not a statement I could've imagined myself uttering back in 1996, but this is different. This is about decent, flavoursome beers being sent off to Cameron's where they are sterile filtered, carbonated, then returned to Toft Green in thirty-litre plastic kegs. I have tasted them and can say, hand on heart, that they're really very good. So I have no hesitation in recommending Legion IX (6.5 per cent) and Imperium (7.5 per cent). I would though urge a word of caution regarding this new 'craft' beer trend. However it is dressed up it is not Cask Ale, beware!

On the down side – at least as far as Smithy and I are concerned – is the lack of any progress, as we see it, on the pubs side. When we went into that area we tapped into an appetite for a new kind of pub in York, and we envisaged expanding at a steady pace. We certainly would have been in there pitching when a prime site, just across the road in the railway station, became available. In fact, Jamie Hawksworth, formerly U.K. sales agent for the Czech brewery Bernard, snapped up the lease and gave us The York Tap. It's wildly successful, and I rarely pass it without reminding myself that the Brewery missed a golden chance.

Seeing the brewery miss out on this and many other opportunities is grievous. Just as hard to take are the comments of old friends and acquaintances who ask me what's happened to our pubs. I don't always know what to say because, having continued to visit them from time to time, I see nothing but decline. However, once it's done it's done. I am not privy to the reasons behind the latest developments and I try not to get engaged in negative talk. Even so, it's hard to avoid that sort of discussion because I still care, deeply.

So where are Smithy and I today? Both in good health. I've managed to kick my habit of sixty a day, and Smithy has reduced his daily consumption drastically – to around forty. He has lived for some years in a small village near Darlington where he has joined the carnival committee, parish council and grows a fine vegetable garden. Tragically, he lost his long-term partner, Trevor, to cancer in 2015 and had to re-structure his life. Between times he puts in a few hours at the village shop and pub, not one for sitting around the house all day.

I continue to visit the brewery and the pubs, where I still know many of the staff – although less so as the years go by. I'm pleased to say that I'm still recognised and well treated, and enjoy a chat while imbibing one of the best beers in the world – and that's official.

LAST ORDERS

When life's troubles weigh you down,
pour yourself a pint and remember
Benjamin Franklin's celebrated words:

*'Beer is God's way of telling us
He wants us to be happy.'*

But you don't need to wait until you're down in
the dumps. I'll raise a glass to it right now.